CHANGE:
THREAT OR OPPORTUNITY
FOR HUMAN PROGRESS?

DEDICATION

The five volumes in this series, the product of a collaborative international effort, are dedicated to all those global citizens committed to serving human progress to the best of their abilities.

CHANGE:
THREAT OR OPPORTUNITY
FOR HUMAN PROGRESS?

Edited by
Üner Kirdar

VOLUME V

ECOLOGICAL CHANGE: ENVIRONMENT, DEVELOPMENT AND POVERTY LINKAGES

United Nations
New York
1992

The contents of this book do not necessarily reflect
the views of the United Nations or of the United Nations Development
Programme. The papers in this volume were contributed by authors in
their personal capacities and they are solely responsible for their views.
Authors are listed with their affiliations at the time of the
Antalya Round Table.

United Nations Publications
United Nations
Room DC2-853
New York, N.Y. 10017, U.S.A.

United Nations Publications
Palais des Nations
1221 Geneva 10
Switzerland

Vol. V
Ecological Change:
Environment, Development and Poverty Linkages
U.N. Sales No. E.91.III.B.9
ISBN 92-1-126028-0

Complete Set (Vol. I–Vol. V):
U.N. Sales No. E.91.III.B.10
ISBN 92-1-126029-9

CONTENTS

Chapter 1

ISSUES
AND QUESTIONS

Üner Kirdar

The interrelated issues of economic development, poverty and environment are emerging as a central item on the agenda of global development challenges for the years ahead. Despite marked progress in improving human well-being over the past three decades, poverty remains as serious as ever. Similarly, severe threats to the global environment and ecological systems caused by over-production, consumption and poverty are rapidly increasing.

There is now a growing awareness among scientists and policy-makers that eliminating global poverty and sustaining the environment are inextricably linked courses of action. Because of a lack of viable economic opportunities, nearly 500 million poor people in the world are at present coerced into meeting their short-term survival needs at the cost of long-term ecological sustainability and the well-being of future generations. Yet, the financial and policy commitments needed to alter this situation tend to lag behind the realization of this state of affairs. In many instances, environmental considerations are still regarded as constraints to development or vice versa.

At present, the major reason for the continuing deterioration of the world ecology and environment is the unsustainable patterns of production and consumption, particularly in industrialized countries. In developing countries, the persistence of poverty and restricted economic opportunities are the main sources of deterioration in the physical environment. Environmental protection in developing countries must therefore be viewed as an integral part of the development process and cannot be considered in isolation from it.

Dangerous changes

As the twentieth century comes to a close, not only are the number of people and their activities vastly increasing, but major unintended global changes are also occurring. If these trends persist, neither human capacity nor technology may have the power, when the twenty-first century begins, to combat radically the deterioration of global systems.

Between 1950 and 1980, the world economy grew threefold, as did the consumption of fossil fuels. The amount of carbon dioxide in the atmosphere increased by 25 per cent. About 95 per cent of the total global carbon dioxide in the atmosphere is at present caused by the combustion of fossil fuels, consumed mostly by the industrialized countries. It is estimated that this consumption, which is nearly 2 billion tons per annum, may rise to over 10 billion tons during the next millennium. As a result of this trend, it is also expected that, by the year 2050, the average temperature of the earth may rise in the range of 1.5°C to 4.5°C. Such an increase is regarded to be sufficient to cause a major worldwide climatic change, which could further exacerbate the existing problems of drought, desertification, soil erosion and could hamper the prospective economic growth of many countries.

Another consequence of global warming is the expansion of the oceans, with a resulting rise in sea levels of a magnitude of 1.4 to 2.2 metres. Since nearly one third of the world's population lives within 60 kilometres of a coastline, such an occurrence would have a profound impact on patterns of agricultural growth, industry, transport and habitation.

On a global basis, at present, the world's forests are disappearing at a rate of 15 million hectares each year, with most of the losses occurring in humid parts of all regions. With the present rate of deforestation, about 40 per cent of the remaining forest cover in all developing countries may be lost by the year 2000. Two fifths of Africa's non-desert land risks being turned into deserts, as does one third of that in Asia and one fifth of that in Latin America. Already, acid precipitation and other forms of industrial air pollution have damaged more than 12 thousand square miles, one fifth of the total temperate forested areas in Europe. The rapid destruction of tropical rain forests does not occur only because of the survival needs of poor people living nearby, but also because of increasing demand patterns of industrialized countries and exorbitant external debt payments. In importing industrialized countries, the consumption of tropical hardwoods has risen to 15 times the level of the 1950s as compared to three times in producing developing countries. The overcutting of forests also causes the loss of numerous species and genetic resources, as well as increases in soil erosion and downstream flooding. It is estimated that over the next 25 years, at least two million species will be in danger of extinction.

The point is that the longer these circumstances persist, the higher the risks and remedial costs will be as well as the impact on the economic and social life of billions of people.

Historical development

Environmental degradation is not a new issue. It has occurred since the start of the Industrial Revolution, two centuries ago. Until recently, the prevailing notion in developed countries was that the effects of industrial pollution should be disregarded, as long as industry generated enough jobs. In this context, it may also be noted that modern society developed on the basis of two faulty perceptions and assumptions: first, natural resources are not finite; secondly, nature can cope with any degree of human interference resulting from unlimited economic growth.

Environmental concerns and their influence on society and national economy began in the industrialized countries only in the late 1960s, because of national and regional problems. Contrary to some beliefs, the initial international consciousness of environmental problems and their possible impact did not arise in the industrialized countries of the West, but in Eastern Europe. The question was brought to international attention for the first time in April 1967 by Czechoslovakia and Poland, in the context of the work of the United Nations Economic Commission for Europe. Being affected by the acid rain and industrial pollution generated mainly by the Federal Republic of Germany, these countries proposed the convening in 1969 of a meeting of European governmental experts to study the problems relating to the environment and their influence on society. At that time, paradoxically, the proposal was adopted after serious doubts and questioning by the Western European countries. It was only two years later, on 30 July 1968, that the Economic and Social Council of the United Nations, on the basis of a proposal from Argentina, Kuwait, Mexico, Morocco, Sweden, Turkey and the United States, recommended to the General Assembly to convene in 1972 a United Nations conference on problems of the human environment.

The first United Nations Conference on the Human Environment, held in Stockholm in 1972, laid down, inter alia the following principles:

> "Economic and social development was essential for ensuring a favourable living and working environment for man and for creating conditions on earth that were necessary for the improvement of the quality of life.
>
> Environmental deficiencies generated by the conditions of underdevelopment and natural disasters posed grave problems and could best be remedied by accelerated development through the transfer of substantial quantities of financial and technological assistance as a supplement to the domestic efforts of the developing countries and such timely assistance as might be required.
>
> For the developing countries, stability of prices and adequate earnings for primary commodities and raw material were essential to environmental management, since economic factors as well as ecological processes had to be taken into account."

In practice, unfortunately, not only were these principles overlooked, but the development problems of developing countries were only incidentally linked to environmental issues.

North-South differences

It would be a mistake to assume that the perceptions of environmental problems, their origins and their impact on development are identical for the industrial countries of the North and for the developing countries of the South.

Many environmental problems in the North are regarded as consequences of affluence. In truth, the environmental problems of the North are the result of overdevelopment, extravagant consumption of fossil fuels, and unrestrained demands for ever-larger quantities of goods and services.

Environmental degradation in the developing countries of the South is regarded frequently as a symptom, or an end product, of poverty, not of affluence. A rapidly growing population puts pressure on the natural resources of a country. The increasing demands for food and basic energy needs for cooking and heating result in the destruction of forests, degradation of the soil, and the depletion of water supplies. Most of the sub-Saharan African countries can be cited as prime examples of this phenomenon. These countries are deficient mostly in usable energy resources. The largest part of their populations, until recently, were rural people, mostly farming families, who, for numerous reasons, are now becoming migrants and urban poor. In addition to climatic changes and soil desertification, the crash in world prices of agricultural commodities is robbing most of the farmers of the South of their jobs. They do not benefit, as in the case of the North, from governmental subsidies, regulations and social security. Similarly, new discoveries in biotechnology are drastically changing the form of agricultural production. The farmers of the South neither possess, not are knowledgeable of such technologies. These factors drive millions of people to cut down the rain forests in order to meet their daily survival and energy needs, thereby creating a human desertification of rural areas just as damaging as soil desertification. Thus, those who possess neither the physical and human capital, nor the means of production, often have no other choice but to exploit the natural resources to which they have access. The end result—poverty—becomes the major source of physical environmental deterioration and ecological depletion.

In a political environment where short-term interests normally dominate long-term concerns, it is not easy for impoverished people to understand, let alone to accept readily, the virtues of undertaking the necessary measure for environmental and ecological conservation. Such demands are regarded as another "conditionality" imposed by the North on their developmental undertakings, similar to the structural adjustment packages of the early 1980s.

The characteristics

In the context of global development challenges for the years ahead, the issue of environment and development presents three distinct characteristics, when compared with other issues identified above.

First, environment and development is at present one of those very rare subjects on which there is consensus among both industrialized and developing countries: all agree that global action and cooperation is required. Concrete proof of this is shown by General Assembly resolution 44/228, which was adopted unanimously on 22 December 1989, and by which was convened the United Nations Conference on Environment and Development. Thus, in a period of declining multilateralism in developmental cooperation, but increasing collaboration in the political arena, this could be regarded as a concrete example of recognition that global security also has economic, social and environmental dimensions no less demanding of attention than political and military ones.

Secondly, the re-emergence of environment and development as a major global challenge for the 1990s, is not the result of governmental foresight and leadership. It is the end result of strong lobbying efforts on the parts of non-governmental organizations, constituencies of national conservationists, media networks and international think-tanks, such as the Brundtland Commission. These are the movements which revived the environmental concerns of the early 1970s, and influenced governments to embark upon a new joint undertaking. These are the forces which generated the present growing awareness that higher growth and eradication of poverty are equally essential to the preservation of the environment.

Thirdly, the emerging conception that environment and development are very closely linked shows that the world is increasingly confronted with issues that affect people as a whole. It also shows that most of these issues are interlinked and multidimensional. They cannot be solved by fragmented sectoral or national approaches alone. Their solutions require multidisciplinary joint undertakings.

Until very recently, both debate and international cooperative efforts have been limited to certain aspects of the environmental problems involved, such as air and water pollution; erosion and other forms of soil deterioration; secondary effects of biocides; and waste. Finally, it is recognized today that many of the environmental issues transcend individual countries and threaten the entire world's ecological and economic system, for example, the warming of the planet from the emission of carbon dioxide into the atmosphere—the so-called green house effect—and the threat from the depletion of the ozone layer. These issues require global action.

There are also many environmental issues that affect several countries, but not necessarily all. They are, therefore, international in character, without being thereby always global. In this category, one may cite the following examples: pollution of fresh water and international rivers; acid rain; nuclear waste; deforestation; erosion of soils; flooding of river basins and plains; and expanding deserts.

More importantly, there is now a clear cognizance of the strong causal relationships between environmental and developmental issues. Environmental damage can no longer be corrected by the operations of market forces; therefore, the intervention of public action becomes essential. During the last decade, the growing emphasis on cost reduction in the increasingly harsh competitive international business world also led to the occurrence of a number of major industrial accidents and natural disasters which have seriously affected human life and economic conditions in many countries. These events brought to the forefront the need to take effective and appropriate measures in risk management, both at national and international levels.

A new agenda

In the light of the above, there is now a broad consensus on a large series of issues which could constitute an agenda for the global development challenge for the years ahead in the environment and development area. These issues are:

- Protection of the atmosphere, combating climate change, depletion of the ozone later, and transboundary air pollution;

- Sound management of waste, particularly hazardous waste and toxic chemicals, prevention of illegal international traffic in toxic and dangerous products and wastes;

- Protection of the quality and supply of fresh water resources;

- Combat against desertification, drought and deforestation;

- Protection of the seas and oceans, and of their living resources;

- Combat against soil degradation;

- Conservation of biological diversity and the sound management of biotechnology;

- A more integrated approach to environment and development problems;

- Sounder management of the pattern of production and consumption;

- Eradication of poverty and improvement of the living and working environment of the poor in urban slums and rural area;

• Protection of human health conditions and the improvement of the quality of life.

Questions

In the light of the above analysis, a number of questions arise in connection with environment and development as an important agenda item of global development challenges in the years ahead.

What are the true chances of translating the newly growing awareness of close interlinkages between the issues of economic growth, poverty and environment to concrete policy actions and increased international financial assistance?

Will environmental concerns dominate international development policies in the near future, or vice versa, will development requirements and poverty eradication concerns lead over environmental planning and management?

Will the present environmental concerns in industrialized countries generate additional sources of international assistance? Or will it simply divert the present limited financial development assistance resources to purely environmental protection projects? Will environmental and ecological conservation requirements become another "conditionality package" imposed by donor countries and/or multilateral financing agencies on recipients for their development undertakings?

What type of concrete measure need to be taken to alert effective policy-makers and, in developing countries, force them to take necessary actions in order to alter radically the present trends and causes of serious environmental deterioration, such as the overcutting of rain forests, soil and water erosion, and urban migration? How to convince these policy-maker that short-term political interests and physical development concerns should not mortgage the long-term development viabilities of their countries and the future of their coming generations?

What will be needed to ensure that environmental considerations are no longer seen as constraints to development? What can be done, so that, on the contrary, the protection of the environment and ecological systems can be a spur to development through the search for new technologies, new way of doing things and new resources to remove the sources of pollution that stem from underdevelopment and poverty?

What lessons can one learn from the forces that generated the recent revival of environmental concerns and forced the governments of industrialized countries to take the necessary action to achieve the same success in multilateral development cooperation?

Chapter 2

REQUIRED GLOBAL CHANGES: CLOSE LINKAGES BETWEEN ENVIRONMENT AND DEVELOPMENT

Maurice Strong*

The unprecedented increase in human numbers and activities since the Industrial Revolution, particularly in this century, have given rise to a deterioration of the environment and depletion of natural resources that threaten the future of the planet. It is ironic that these impacts have occurred largely as a result of the same processes that have produced such unparalleled levels of wealth and prosperity, particularly in the industrialized world.

At the centre of the current dilemma is the gross imbalance that has been created by the concentration of economic growth in the industrialized countries and population growth in the developing countries. Redressing this imbalance will be the key to the future security of our planet in environmental, economic, and traditional security terms. This will require fundamental changes in both our economic behaviour and our international relations. Effecting these changes peacefully and co-operatively is, without doubt, the principal challenge of our time.

*Secretary-General of the United Nations Conference on Environment and Development, 1992. This paper is based on several speeches delivered by Mr. Strong and edited by Üner Kirdar for this book.

In this important undertaking, cooperation can be based only on common interests. While there is widespread acknowledgement, at the level of the principle of the need to achieve a sustainable balance between environment and development, it should be no surprise that the perspectives of developing countries on the issues differ substantially from those of industrialized countries. Developing countries point out that the industrialized countries are largely responsible for these risks and have been the main beneficiaries of the wealth that has accumulated through the processes of economic growth. They insist that they cannot divert resources required to meet the most immediate and fundamental needs of the people, to pay the additional costs of incorporating into their development policies and practices the measures needed to reduce major global risks. At the same time, they ask that the industrialized nations take seriously the compelling case made by the Brundtland Commission that the common need for global environmental security requires a substantial and sustained increase in the flow of financial resource to support the broad development needs of developing countries, with particular priority to a massive attack on poverty.

Developing countries and environmental issues

When environment first emerged as a global concern in the late 1960s and early 1970s, it was the industrialized countries that placed it on the international agenda and took the initiative in convening the United Nations Conference on the Human Environment, held in Stockholm in 1972. The environment issue was initially seen, somewhat narrowly, as a disease of the rich, an unintended by-product of the processes of economic growth that had produced for them such unprecedented levels of wealth and prosperity.

Developing countries saw this new preoccupation by the rich with environment as a new constraint on their own development. They insisted that the environment agenda and dialogue be broadened to accommodate their concerns and the issues of poverty, underdevelopment, natural resources and inequity, which are intimately and inextricably bound up with environmental conditions and prospects in their countries.

The recognition of the essential linkages between environment and development was a dominant theme of the Stockholm Conference in 1972. But all too little progress was made towards the actual integration of the environmental dimension into development policies and practices until the 1987 World Commission on Environment and Development, in its report "Our Common Future", gave new impetus to this process. It documented, in compelling terms, the case for sustainable development—the full integration of environment and development-as the only sound and viable means of ensuring both our environment and development futures. It made clear that the transition to sustainable development is equally imperative for both developing and more industrialized countries, while the vastly different conditions under which they must make this transition impose special handicaps on the poor and special responsibilities on the rich.

General Assembly resolution 44/228, which established the mandate of the United Nations Conference on Environment and Development, to be held in Brazil in June 1992, made it clear that this is indeed to be a conference on "environment and development" and that environment and development must be considered on an integrated basis in every aspect of the Conference's agenda.

Environmental problems of the developing countries

Most of the developing countries have in many respects become the victims, rather than the beneficiaries, of the recent globalization of the world economy. Interdependence has made their fragile economies highly vulnerable to changes in the world economic conditions, over which they have no control. It compels them to compete in an international market-place in which the principal sources of added value and comparative advantage are technology, capital, management and marketing skills and scientific knowledge. In all of these areas, the developing countries are seriously handicapped. They are often compelled to overexploit the natural resources on which their development future depends.

For the developing countries, environmental degradation means deterioration in the quality and supply of fresh water, depletion of renewable sources of energy, destruction of forests, and deterioration and loss of productive soil. In most of these countries, the result is a serious and accelerating deterioration of the carrying capacity of the principal resource and ecological systems on which development and survival depend. The growing numbers of poor who are driven from the land to seek refuge in the cities and towns add to the pressures on these equally vulnerable urban systems. Most cannot keep up with the need to provide safe water supplies, health services and job opportunities. Thus, ecological deterioration translates quickly into economic decline and human suffering for fragile economies that are already heavily burdened by debt, unfavourable terms of trade, dependency on external supplies of food and energy and which have inadequate infrastructure, institutional and professional capacities. The great African famine of 1984 and 1985 was as much a product of the interaction between ecological breakdown and economic recession as it was of the extended period of drought that afflicted much of sub-Saharan Africa.

The developing countries require substantially increased assistance to enable them to build stronger and more diversified economies, to effect the transition to sustainable development and to reduce their vulnerability to changes in the international economy. This requires, first and foremost, that they be helped to break the vicious circle of ecological deterioration and economic decline and adopt environmentally sound patterns of natural resource use and agricultural production. They should be especially encouraged and supported in their effort to upgrade their capacity to add value to the natural resources and commodities on which they depend primarily for their export earnings.

The development of their strengths and the reduction of their vulnerabilities require a quantum increase in support for the development of their human resources and related institutional capacities, particularly in the fields of science, technology, management and professional skills. Traditional patterns of technical assistance which often deepen dependence on foreign experts are simply not adequate. What is needed is a sustained commitment to building indigenous human and institutional capacities. This is the indispensable prerequisite to breaking out of the present deeply entrenched patterns of environmental economic deterioration, dependency and vulnerability.

It is of critical importance that this be done on a basis that combines traditional and modern knowledge and methods. Human and institutional development which alienates people from traditional values and sources of knowledge will be counterproductive and often socially destructive. The best and most sustainable development is that in which the processes and techniques of modernization are assimilated sensitively into existing social and value systems without destroying or undermining them.

The UNDP landmark report *Human Development 1990* articulates in especially clear and persuasive terms the importance of giving priority to human resources. Also, the UNDP initiative in establishing sustainable development networks in developing countries offers a promising framework for giving new impetus to the development of indigenous human and institutional capacity. The need to develop this capacity in each country is as critically important from the point of view of environmental protection as it is of development: it is the indispensable key to sustainable development.

The economic crisis which continues to confront the developing countries provides a unique opportunity to break with the traditional development modes that have produced the current impasse and establish a new development model expressing basic values, needs and interests while at the same time building on its unique endowment of natural and human resources. Indeed, such a change is imperative.

Personally, I hope that the 1992 Conference will produce a new political commitment to a global war on poverty as a central priority of the world community in the remainder of the 1990s and into the 21st century. This special attention to the poor and to the developing countries is necessary because, contrary to much conventional wisdom, the integration of environment and development is, if anything, even more urgent for those caught up in the vicious circle of poverty than for those countries at more advanced stages of economic development. It is not a matter that can be postponed until development has reached a later stage; rather, it is the prerequisite for the revitalization of development. It is the developing countries most of all that have the greatest and most immediate need to effect the transition to sustainable development. They are most vulnerable to the environmental degradation which destroys their natural capital as well as adding to such global risks as climate change. Environmental vulnerability thus compounds and exacerbates their economic vulnerability.

Recent evolution of environmental problems in the industrialized countries

Since the Stockholm Conference, too little has been done to give practical effect to the integration of environment and development in economic policy and decision-making. While a great deal of progress was made towards environmental improvement in particular instances, the Brundtland Commission made it clear that, overall, the environment of our planet has deteriorated since 1972 and there has been a serious acceleration of such major environmental risks as ozone depletion and global warming.

The evolution of the environment as an important public issue in the 1970s was accompanied by the establishment of environmental agencies and ministries by virtually all Governments. While some, like the United States Environmental Protection Agency, were given formidable powers, they were primarily in the areas of review and regulation. Environmental agencies and ministries had little influence on economic policy or the policies or practices of the major sectoral agencies, the activities of which are the principal sources of environmental impacts. The result has been an over-reliance on regulation. We are now experiencing, and in some cases are already exceeding, the practical limits of regulation. Regulation is, of course, necessary but experience has demonstrated that its effects can be limited, and sometimes negative, if it is not accompanied by changes in economic and fiscal policies which provide positive incentives for environmentally sound and sustainable economic development.

In all countries, the fiscal system has provided incentives and subsidies designed to meet a wide variety of political and public policy objectives usually unrelated to environmental considerations, many of which have become deeply entrenched and difficult to change. Agricultural subsidies are a prime example. We now realize that many of these, in addition to their economic cost and the distortions they create in the market economy, also provide incentives for environmentally unsound economic practices. Governments must therefore undertake an extensive review and reorientation of the system of incentives and penalties which motivate the economic behaviour of corporations and individuals, to ensure that they provide positive incentives for environmentally sound and sustainable behaviour.

The changes which these measures must be designed to achieve will be fundamental and pervasive in nature. They will affect virtually every sector of industry, particularly those which are resource-based, such as energy, forestry, mining and business, those which produce products that have significant potential for environmental impact, such as the chemical and packaging industries and those heavily based on the use of fossil fuels in the automobile and transport industries. This will involve significant changes in lifestyles as more people in the industrialized world opt for lives of sophisticated modesty and people of developing countries receive greater support in their attempts to achieve livelihoods which do not undermine or destroy the environment and resource base on which their future livelihoods depend. There will be basic changes in consumer preferences and practices, the portents of which are already visible in the move towards green consumerism.

These changes will have an effect on the structure of industry and relationships between industry and society, as profound as anything that has taken place since the industrial revolution; indeed, they add up to a veritable "eco-industrial revolution", in which environmental considerations will more and more drive economic policy and industrial transformation.

All this may seem an overimaginative and perhaps even unrealistic extrapolation from current realities, in which preoccupation with immediate economic pressures and political concerns pre-empt the attention of both political and business leaders. But if the movement towards more environmentally sound and sustainable economic behaviour is temporarily overshadowed by such immediate preoccupations, it will soon force its way back to the centre of the agenda. For if our diagnosis is right, it represents a fundamental transition in human affairs that is already well under way and will be seen in the perspective of history as the main source of the forces shaping our future in the twenty-first century and beyond. It is, of course, inextricably linked with the unprecedented political, economic and technological changes that are transforming our world into a single, interdependent planetary society. It is always more difficult to appreciate fundamental changes when one is caught up in them. And there is a great deal of evidence that the eco-industrial revolution is already well under way. Let us take for example, the experience of industrialized countries in reducing the energy and materials content of industrial production. Japan provides the most impressive example, having reduced the energy use required to produce a unit of gross domestic product (GDP) by some 40 per cent since 1975, while effecting during the same period a reduction of the raw materials component by a similar proportion. Quite apart from the environmental advantages, this is said to give Japanese products an economic competitive advantage of something like 5 per cent in the United States market—as compared with products of a similar nature produced in the United States. In this period also, Japanese industry developed a new competitive advantage in pollution control and environmentally benign industrial processes as the result of a combination of some of the strictest air and water pollution regulations in the world, coupled with generous incentives to its industry.

Japan's experience has demonstrated that environmental improvement is fully compatible with high rates of economic performance and can indeed make a positive contribution to performance. At the other extreme, the experience of the Soviet Union and countries of Eastern and Central Europe is that some of the worst examples of environmental neglect and deterioration have been the by-products of equally disastrous economic management and performance.

There is no question that the kind of transition we are making to an environmentally driven economy will create significant problems and disruptions for many. However, I believe that the experience of Japan and others has already demonstrated that such changes can produce at least as many new opportunities as new problems for business. There is further evidence for this, in the fact that such environmentally related industries as waste management and pollution control are now among the best performing growth industries.

Interdependence and sustainable development

Interdependence is not an unmitigated blessing, particularly when it serves to exacerbate the vulnerability of the weak and increase their dependence on events they cannot control. The international economic environment has clearly contributed to the gross imbalances between North and South that have weakened the economies of developing countries during the past decade. These imbalances continue to present a primary barrier to the revitalization of the economies of these countries and to their prospects for effecting the transition to sustainable development.

It is now clear that the transition to sustainability is the only means of ensuring the revitalization of the development process, which is the key to the future of all developing countries. It is also clear that the patterns of development that have evolved during this century, based largely on the wasteful and destructive development model of the North, will not meet the human, developmental or environmental needs of the twenty-first century. Industrialized countries themselves must move beyond this model.

Population is a critical element in the environment-development equation. The relationship between population dynamics and ecosystems is decisive in achieving sustainable development. Demographic factors stemming from rates and distribution of population growth will be a primary determinant in the transition to sustainability. Each country must determine the relationship between, on the one hand, the growth and distribution of its own population, its environment and resource base and, on the other hand, the level and quality of life its development policies and programmes are designed to produce for its people. Nevertheless, an overall reduction in population growth and the early achievement of population stability are imperative.

Sustainable development cannot be imposed by external pressures; it must be rooted in the culture, the values, the interests and the priorities of the people concerned. While the transition to sustainability will require a supportive international economic environment, it must not provide a basis for the external imposition of new conditions or constraints on development. Developing countries cannot be denied their right to grow, nor to choose their own pathways to growth.

At the same time, the transition of developing countries to sustainability cannot be expected without the support of the international community. This is particularly needed to reverse the outflow of resources that has stifled the economic growth of the developing countries and to ensure that these countries have access on a long-term basis to the resource flows they will need to revitalize their economic life and make the transition to environmentally sustainable development. Of critical importance in this is the need to deal more fundamentally with the debt issue. Debt-for-nature swaps may be useful in addressing particular needs but are marginal in their overall effect. The principle behind them may, however, serve as a basis for the kind of radical reduction in debt-servicing charges that is essential to the revitalization of development.

Sustainable development involves a process of deep and profound change in the political, social, economic, institutional and technological order, including the redefinition of relations between developing and more developed countries. Governments must take the lead and establish the basic policy framework incentives and infrastructures required for sustainability. However, the primary actors are people, acting through the many non-governmental organizations and citizen groups through which societies function. The 1992 United Nations Conference on Environment and Development—The Earth Summit— can succeed only if it has a sound base in the awareness and engagement of people.

Need for new global actions

The industrialized countries must take the lead in effecting this transformation, for the unparalleled economic growth that has produced their wealth and power has also given rise to most of the major global environmental risks we face. Developing countries share these risks but are only at the early stages of the economic development to which they aspire. They must grow if they are to develop. But their growth will clearly add immensely to global environmental pressures and risks unless they, too, can make the transition to more sustainable modes of development. They can neither afford to do this, nor be expected to unless they have access to the additional financial resources and technologies they require to integrate the environmental dimension into their development. It is clearly in the interests of the richer countries to help them do so.

This will call for something much more than a mere extension of existing concepts of foreign aid, which can no longer be seen as a satisfactory basis for relationships between rich and poor countries. It calls for a wholly new global partnership based on mutual interest and mutual need, one in which developing countries will have the incentive and the means to cooperate fully in protecting the global environment while meeting their needs and aspirations for economic growth. It will call for new and innovative means to reduce the drain on their resources resulting from intolerable debt burdens and capital outflows and to increase substantially their access to the additional sources of capital required to finance their needs on a sustainable basis.

The stakes are high—nothing less than the survival of our planet as a sustainable home for our species and the other forms of life that inhabit it. The changes we must make in our economic life and our international relations are fundamental in nature and will be extremely difficult to achieve. But the fact that they are imperative provides a powerful incentive to mobilize, on an unprecedented scale, our capacities for political, economic and social innovation and leadership. This must be manifested at every level—from the behaviour of individuals to global cooperation.

Most actions, even on such major global risks as climate change, must be taken at the national as well as the local levels. The integrated nature of the global economy and the imperatives of competitiveness require that even actions with primary impact at the local level must be taken in a global context.

Thus, for example, increasing traffic congestion and air pollution in major urban areas such as Los Angeles provide incentives for a reduction in the use of fossil fuels which, in turn, will reinforce efforts to reduce the risk of global climate change. In many cases, agreement at the global level on basic principles, criteria and targets will be necessary to provide the context for national and local action.

Conclusions

The 1992 Conference will focus largely on the changes we must make in our economic behaviour and economic relations to ensure global environmental security. The rich countries must clearly show the necessary leadership in this transition. It is they who have developed and benefited from the traditional development model that has produced our present dilemma—and they are the only ones with the means and the power to change it. It will be no easy task. Inertia is as powerful a force in human affairs as it is in the physical world. Although the transition to sustainable development will ultimately produce more opportunities, and certainly more benefits, than continuing "business as usual" along the traditional growth pathway, the processes of change themselves will inevitably be disruptive, and there will be strong resistance from those most immediately threatened by them.

The transition to sustainability requires much more effective use of resources and accountability for the environmental as well as the economic impact of such use. This must depend primarily on the provision of the necessary incentives to change rather than to rely too much on regulatory measures. The operation of market forces can and must be a powerful ally in providing the incentives to change. It is, after all, fully consistent with market economy principles that every economic transaction and product must absorb the full costs to which it gives rise, including environmental costs.

No single event can be expected in itself to resolve the many complex issues that will be confronting the world community in Rio de Janeiro in 1992. However, the Conference offers a unique opportunity to provide the basis for the major shift in inertia required to put us on the pathway to a more secure and sustainable future. At the core of this shift there will be changes in our economic life, a more careful and more caring use of the earth's resources and greater cooperation and equity in sharing the benefits as well as the risks of our technological civilization. Similarly, the Conference must provide a new basis for relations between rich and poor, North and South, including a concerted attack on poverty as a central priority for the twenty-first century. This is now as imperative in terms of our environmental security as it is in moral and humanitarian terms.

This will require basic changes in attitudes, values and social priorities as well as in the development of the necessary scientific, technological and professional skills. There will undoubtedly be a continued need for more specialization in scientific education and training. There must be much greater emphasis on the capacity to understand and deal with the economic, social and public policy impacts of scientific and technological change. Of particular importance is the need to integrate the ecological dimension into education and economics. Economics must truly become economics.

The kinds of changes needed in the industrialized countries to discipline their wasteful and indulgent patterns of production and consumption are very different from the changes needed to overcome poverty and deprivation in developing countries. Nevertheless, fundamental changes are essential in both if we are to make the transition to a more secure and sustainable world community in the twenty-first century. The industrialized countries must lead the processes of change in their own societies and support them in developing countries. In pursuing the concept of "only one Earth", the primary responsibility for our common future is in a very real sense in our own hands.

Chapter 3

POVERTY, ENVIRONMENT AND DEVELOPMENT

Carl Tham*

This paper presents the views of the Swedish International Development Agency (SIDA) on the connections between poverty, environment and development.

The environment was brought to the top of the international agenda in the 1980s. The appearance of the global threats of acidification, ozone-layer depletion and climatic change meant an enormous increase in the interest and resources devoted to environmental problems. There is now an increasing awareness among policy-makers worldwide that policies have to change in order to ensure a sustainable development in the developed as well as the developing world. However, the need for concrete action is urgent.

As a result of the somewhat different ecological conditions and a considerably faster population growth, the environmental problems in developing countries are more serious today than they were at the corresponding stage in the development process of the industrial countries. Environmental problems are already threatening the survival of large numbers of people in the developing world and these problems are becoming increasingly more serious. The degradation of the environment in the developing countries is especially disturbing since these countries have very small resources to counteract the negative effects of

*Director-General of the Swedish International Development Agency, Stockholm.

degradation. Nevertheless, it is essential that these effects are counter-acted. Developing countries, and in particular the poorest people in these countries, must achieve economic betterment in a way that also works in the long run—a sustainable development. The developed countries must assist the developing countries in this process.

Even though the environmental problems of the developing countries are the subject of an increasingly intensive and well-informed discussion, it is not always the case that the connection with poverty is made clear. The number of very poor people is increasing, especially in Africa, and the gap between the rich and the poor is growing in many places. More than one billion people live in poverty—approximately one-third of the population of the developing world. At the same time, the problem of environmental degradation is growing in many poor areas.

SIDA is currently in the process of analysing the links between environmental degradation and poverty. This paper presents conclusions of this work and outlines some of the strategic changes in programmes of development cooperation that are needed to address these problems.

Poverty and environmental degradation are connected in two ways. First, poverty is often a *result* of environmental degradation. Soil erosion, deforestation, water pollution, the loss of flora and fauna and so on, all have a negative impact on the production possibilities of individuals and societies, with varying degrees of poverty as a consequence. For the individual, the result can be dramatic—millions of people are classified as environmental refugees. For society as a whole, poverty is seen as a reduction in the stock of natural resources and as an increase in the cost of mitigating the negative effects.

Secondly, poverty is often a *cause* of environmental degradation. Extreme poverty often means limited knowledge as well as a lack of resources to make the investments necessary to protect the environment. It is, for example, often the case that the poor waste energy—with environmental degradation as a result—because they do not have access to modern, efficient technologies.

However, the connection between poverty and the environment must not be oversimplified. There are many examples of extremely poor people, measured by traditional standards, who do not destroy the environment in which they live. Likewise, there are countless examples of rich people and societies who devastate their own environment.

The consequences of environmental degradation for the poor are often obvious, although they are not well documented. However, the few systematic studies that have been carried out do not provide a clear-cut picture of poverty as a cause of environmental degradation. The relationship is complex not least on account of the fact that both poverty and environmental degradation are multidimensional concepts that are difficult to define. Thus, more research will be necessary before a clearer picture emerges. It is, nevertheless, possible to point out a number of links between poverty and environmental degradation. The significance of these links is not entirely clear and is likely to vary according to the environmental problem being considered, in different geographical areas and at different points in time. It seems fruitless to search for simple, universally applicable links between poverty and the environment.

Links between poverty and the environment

It is clear that environmental degradation contributes to a considerable extent to poverty in the Third World. This takes place directly, for example when the pollution of land, water and air causes health problems, and indirectly when environmental degradation reduces the productive potential of land and water resources. Environmental degradation in the form of soil erosion, desertification, deforestation, over-fishing, the disappearance of species of flora and fauna, the pollution of the air, land and water, the salinization of irrigated land and so on, affect negatively the production potential for poor people in both rural and urban areas. Environmental degradation also exposes the poorest people to greater risks for natural disasters and famine. Thus, for example, the famine disasters in Ethiopia and the floods in Bangladesh in the 1980s had their roots in extensive environmental degradation. During recent years, the concept "environmental refugee" has been coined. Millions of people, mainly in Africa, but also in other parts of the world have fled from their homes because nature can no longer feed them.

In many areas where poverty still persists or is growing, sometimes despite a generally satisfactory economic development, for example, in India and Kenya, the stress on the ecological systems is increasing. The poorest 20 per cent in developing countries comprises 780 million people (1988), of which 390 million live in South Asia and 156 million people in Africa. Of these 780 million people, some 470 million, or 60 per cent, live in areas severely threatened by environmental degradation.

Deforestation, soil erosion and desertification have already reached catastrophic levels in several places in the developing world and the situation is deteriorating at an ever-increasing pace. For example, the forests in certain densely populated countries in West Africa and Central America will completely disappear by the year 2000 if current trends continue. In India, almost 40 per cent of agricultural land is affected by erosion. The Food and Agricultural Organization of the United Nations (FAO) has estimated that agricultural production will decrease by 25 per cent in many developing countries between the years 1975 and 2000 if no measures are taken to conserve the soil. If these trends are not reversed, poverty and human suffering in the countries concerned will increase.

Lack of water is a problem in many poor developing countries. There is a great danger that the situation—particularly for the poor, who already have the greatest difficulty in obtaining water—will deteriorate in countries in which access to clean water is diminishing as a result of pollution and overconsumption. Ethiopia, Kenya, Somalia and parts of Botswana are examples of areas where there is already a serious lack of water.

The marine environment is threatened in many places in the world. The pace of degradation of the marine environment has been underestimated, as have its consequences for the development of large groups of people. Overexploitation and pollution of marine resources particularly affect poor fishing communities and others living on the coast and in many places threaten to upset seriously the ecological balance in seas and lakes.

The salinization of irrigated land is a growing problem. The FAO has estimated that 45 million hectares of irrigated land, or almost 50 per cent of the 92 million hectares under irrigation in developing countries, are threatened by salinization.

Developing countries are also threatened by the global environmental problems. Climatic change and the rise in sea levels—conceivable consequences of the greenhouse effect—threaten to affect the poor developing countries more severely than the industrial countries. Also, it is often the poorest people in these countries that are the most exposed to this threat since they live in ecologically sensitive areas and seldom have the resources to protect themselves against a negative external influence.

Industrial pollution in developing countries is a growing problem. Already, emissions are considerable in certain places. The poor are affected directly and indirectly. They are exposed to health risks because they often live in areas close to the source of the emission. They are also affected because the deposition of pollutants reduces the productivity in fishing and farming. Many industries use old technologies which pose a severe threat to the environment. If there is no transition to less polluting technologies, further industrialization in developing countries—which is important in itself—can lead to catastrophic consequences for the environment and for the poor.

At the same time, there is a connection in the other direction. Poverty is a contributory cause of environmental degradation because of several factors outlined below.

- Poverty implies a lack of productive resources. The conservation of the environment often requires resources in the form of capital and labour. For a family living in extreme poverty, it is difficult to spare these resources, because it entails great sacrifices in terms of present consumption possibilities. Therefore, measures to protect the environment—measures whose positive effects often can be seen only at a much later stage and sometimes accrue mainly to others—tend to be given low priority by the very poor. Poverty contributes to short-term thinking.

The tendency to neglect the environment is reinforced by the fact that many poor people do not have the possibility to borrow money to finance investments in environmental protection. Similarly, because of their low credit-worthiness, many poor countries suffer from a shortage of foreign exchange, which is often needed to finance the import of more efficient and environmentally sound technologies. Thus, lack of capital means that poor people and nations may be constrained from protecting the environment even when this would lead to short-term economic gains.

The shortage of land, caused by population growth—itself often a consequence of poverty—and the uneven distribution of land lead to an expansion of cultivation in ecologically sensitive areas in developing countries. The poor, landless people are forced to cultivate these areas since they have no other alternative. It is considered that some 60 per cent of all households in rural areas in developing countries have access to too little land to support themselves at a reasonable level. It appears that this percentage is increasing.

• Poverty often means limited knowledge. Poverty is often characterized by a strong dependence on traditional methods and a lack of information and knowledge about alternative methods of cultivation. In situations where the growth of population forces people to adapt their traditional methods, this lack of knowledge can constitute a serious obstacle to adaptation to methods which are ecologically sound. This is especially true in a rapidly changing world.

- Poverty often means very limited political influence. Even in those cases where they are acutely conscious of the consequences of environmental degradation, poor people seldom have the possibility to influence the political decision-makers, who in many cases actively contribute to, or at least accept, environmental degradation.

The quantitative significance of the ways in which poverty contributes to environmental degradation in developing countries is unknown but it is conceivable that it does so to a considerable extent. One characteristic of the link between environmental degradation and poverty is that they mutually reinforce each other—they are part of a vicious circle. Environmental degradation today leads to greater poverty and therefore to a greater tendency to degrade the environment tomorrow. Thus, the elimination of poverty constitutes, in many cases, a precondition for the elimination of environmental degradation. Similarly, the elimination of environmental degradation is often essential if poverty is to be relieved.

It should, however, be emphasized that the eradication of poverty is not a sufficient condition for solving the environmental problems of developing countries. Poverty is only one of a number of contributory factors behind the environmental degradation in these countries. As long as the other factors are not eliminated, people—both rich and poor—in developing countries will continue to destroy their environment. These factors include:

- Rapid population growth. Population growth means, all other things being equal, an increase in the utilization of natural resources for human needs;

- Free access to natural resources. Many natural resources can be exploited freely by individuals and companies. This readily leads to overexploitation of the resources since free access means that the costs which arise as a result of overexploitation are not reflected in the economic calculations of the individual or company that use the resources;

- Bad economic incentives. Taxes, subsidies and other economic policy instruments have a decisive effect on how individuals and companies affect the environment. An imprudent use of these instruments contributes in a decisive way to environmental degradation in developing countries;

- Greed and lust for power. The longing for material benefits over and above those that are necessary as well as lust for power, cowardice and the failure of decision-makers to take responsibility all contribute to the shortsightedness which leads to a nonsustainable resource use;

- Uneven distribution of land. The uneven distribution of land affects the environment in several different ways. First, an uneven distribution tends to lead to increased cultivation of marginal areas that are more sensitive to erosion, especially if there is a general shortage of land. Secondly, there is some evidence to suggest that small farmers have a greater disposition to protect their land against erosion than do farmers owning extensive lands;

- Collective solutions with the absence of individual responsibility. The absence of individual responsibility—for example, in the collective ownership of natural resources—is an important contributory cause of environmental degradation;

- The absence of democratic instruments of control. In countries where there is no democracy or where there is very little democracy, where environmental organizations and the expression of opinion on the environment have been forbidden or have been kept under very strict control, environmental degradation has taken place much more rapidly.

In particular, the rapid population growth must be regarded as a fundamental cause of both environmental degradation and poverty in developing countries. In the absence of rapid technological progress, a permanently growing population means that the pressure on natural resources, as well as poverty, inevitably increase as more and more resources with a low productive potential must be used.

The role of development assistance

It is important to emphasize that the role of development cooperation is catalytic: it contributes to identifying problems and shows what can be done in different areas. Programmes of development cooperation with the right strategic emphasis can have a positive significance for the environment and for the eradication of poverty in developing countries. However, the responsibility for the solution of the problems ultimately rests with the Governments of the developing countries. It is the conscious or unconscious negligence on the part of these Governments that is the most significant cause of environmental degradation and it is only by means of a decisive reorientation of policies in the countries concerned that environmental degradation can be stopped.

At the same time, it is clear that the industrialized countries must be prepared to increase development assistance in the environmental field, not least in order to contribute to solving the international environmental problems—the greenhouse effect, the depletion of the ozone layer and the depletion of rain forests. These problems are more complex than strictly national problems since, in addition to the need for awareness, knowledge and political will, there is also a problem with the international distribution of responsibility. Everyone can agree on the importance of solving these problems but no one seems to be willing to do the lion's share of the work. This applies in particular to the depletion of the rain forests, where the developing countries are required to make great efforts while the benefits accrue to an equally high degree to the industrialized countries. Development cooperation—in the broadest sense of the term—will play an important role in solving this problem. Without external assistance, it is difficult to see how developing countries can be willing to make the investments needed to preserve a sufficient number of the world's rain forests.

While the industrialized countries give development assistance to environmental conservation, they also contribute in various ways to the environmental degradation we see in developing countries. The emission of greenhouse gases into the atmosphere, the dumping of waste in developing countries and the export of prohibited pesticides and insecticides to developing countries are examples of the direct effect industrialized countries have on the environment of developing countries. A comprehensive strategy to support environmental conservation and to combat poverty in developing countries must also include measures in these areas, which lie outside conventional development cooperation.

An important conclusion of the links between environmental degradation and poverty is that there is no general conflict between environmental protection and economic development in developing countries, particularly not where the poorest people are concerned. In many places, environmental degradation constitutes a growing threat to the possibility of poor people to feed themselves. If this environmental degradation is not stopped, there will be even more poverty tomorrow than there is today. If, for example, the productivity of agriculture diminishes because the land is exposed to erosion, it is obviously a fundamental prerequisite for development that this degradation be stopped. There can, however, be a conflict between short-term and long-term measures in a situation with limited resources. Shall we relieve famine today or prevent famine tomorrow. Moreover, this conflict is not confined to environmental protection but is a part of the overall problem of development.

Another important conclusion is that economic growth, stimulated by development assistance, is a necessary condition (but not a sufficient one) for coming to grips with the environmental degradation in the poor countries. Historically, economic growth has often taken place at the expense of rather than for the benefit of the environment. It is, therefore, essential that economic growth, as well as the development projects which contribute to growth, take place within the framework of sustainable development. This means that development must be such that, in the words of the Brundtland Commission, it "meets the needs of the present without compromising the ability of future generations to meet their own needs".

SIDA is currently working to produce a strategy for dealing with the problems of poverty and environmental degradation in developing countries. Some measures which should be included in such a strategy are presented below:

- An increase in the support to family planning in developing countries. Population growth is perhaps the most serious threat to the environment and to the possibility of poor people in the Third World to support themselves. Greater support to family planning is the single most important measure to bring down the birth rate in this part of the world. At present 1.3 per cent of the world's official development assistance goes to the population field. This figure should be increased to 3–4 per cent;

- A substantial expansion of research and experimental activities in the field of agriculture, above all in Africa. The mutual link between poverty and environmental degradation is especially evident where problems of erosion and deforestation in marginal agricultural areas are concerned. It is, therefore, particularly urgent to increase support to research on sustainable methods of cultivation for small farmers in marginal areas. It is also important to increase, by means of research, production in areas with a high potential, since these areas must absorb a considerable amount of labour during coming decades;

- Greater support to education and information. Lack of knowledge and awareness is one of the most important and pervasive causes of environmental degradation, not least those which affect the poorest people in developing countries. It is, therefore, of utmost importance to extend information and education activities relating to environmental issues within all sectors of society;

• Greater support to public administration development in the environmental field. In many areas, there are enormous shortcomings in the capacity to plan and manage the development of society in a more environmentally sound direction. An expansion of certain parts of the administration is therefore of vital significance in developing countries. This should include more support for the production of strategy documents relating to the environment. It should also include building up the capacity to carry out economic analyses of environmental problems. This applies above all to the valuation and pricing of natural resources in both project calculations and in the national accounts. It is of vital importance that environmental costs, so often concealed today, be is made clear to decision-makers. It also applies to the analysis of the connections between economic policy and environmental degradation. It is important that the need to expand the administration in the environmental area be given due attention when the economic reform programmes are drawn up since demands be often made for reductions in the public sector in these programmes;

• Greater support for the marine environment. The rate of degradation of the marine environment has been underestimated as have the consequences for very large groups of people, not least poor fishing communities;

• Contributions to improve the capacity of developing countries to participate in international environmental work. International work concerning the environment under the auspices of multilateral agencies, and in conferences and conventions, will in all probability increase in the future. The capacity of developing countries to participate in this work must be improved;

• The development of a concrete programme for preserving biological diversity. The disappearance of species of flora and fauna affect many poor people directly—they are deprived of food, raw materials, medicine, etc., and sometimes of their whole way of life;

• Greater support to non-governmental organizations (NGOs) in the environmental field. It is important to extend environmental projects outside the public channels in developing countries. NGOs contribute to greater democratic influence on public decisions regarding the environment and often represent considerable advantages in terms of the motivation of grass roots, local credibility and administrative effectiveness.

Chapter 4

THE DELICATE BALANCE BETWEEN ENVIRONMENT AND DEVELOPMENT: THE LATIN AMERICAN EXPERIENCE

Enrique V. Iglesias*

An immense explosion of international sensitivity concerning the environment is taking place at present. There is a tendency to think that this sensitivity is concentrated exclusively in the industrialized countries. This is not so. Anyone who travels through our hemisphere will be forced to admit that environmental protection is no longer the preserve of isolated groups. This is worth emphasizing because we are responding to a perception that is becoming universal in scope.

It is worth reviewing the history behind this process of growing sensitivity. The truth is that there have always been groups in the world who have been concerned about living with and preserving nature.

Conservation is not a new concern

The conservation movements have their roots in the more primitive communities, which, when threatened by a dearth of resources or a hostile environment, had to devise ways of coexisting with nature in an

*President of the Inter-American Development Bank.

intelligent manner that would permit the conservation of the resources in question. Our region had pre-Columbian communities that knew how to coexist with nature and which have left lessons that today are invaluable tools for managing environmental problems. So we are not discovering a new problem. It was already discovered long before us by civilizations that also called our America home. But, in the last 30 or 40 years, two major previously unknown phenomena burst upon the scene: dramatic population growth and the technological revolution, which acknowledged man's unlimited ingenuity and capacity to provide for the social good, but also created growing threats in the environments where they were applied. So, it is not the concern for conservation that is new. What is new is the qualitative dimension of the phenomenon and the way in which these two elements, population and technology, can combine to work against the environment. That is incompatible with sustained long-term development. The awareness of the problem was raised in the international community at the beginning of the 1970s, through the concern of certain groups that were alarmed by the Club of Rome report, which gave the impression that the world was in some imminent danger of using up its natural resources. The Stockholm Conference was in many ways the first collective international response, where a community of nations identified the first common cause—nature itself—and applied to this discovery the potential for action of the entire United Nations system. From that moment on, the list of common causes grew. The Habitat Conference in Vancouver, the Mar del Plata Water Conference, the Conference on New and Renewable Energies in Nairobi, and conferences on topics such as desertification followed. An international awareness had developed from the warning note sounded by the Club of Rome report, which also drew attention to the potential implications of the economic and social development process upon the environment.

New dimensions

Today, the phenomenon has taken a new dimension in that global threats are now appearing, which legitimately concern the very foundations of society. The conservation of the delicate equilibrium that maintains the planet and the possibility of keeping it through the years by making the existence of mankind compatible with the survival of the planet has become a grass-roots concern. There is a renewed interest that finds expression in initiatives that we are all familiar with: the Brundtland Report; the United Nations Conference on Environment and Development (UNCED) to be held in 1992; the initiatives that governments are taking in our hemisphere; the recent meeting of ministers from Amazonian nations in Quito; and the conference of the Heads of State of the same countries in Manaus to work out a policy of cooperative action that favours Amazonia. All these are indications of what we could term a new awakening of ecological awareness in the international community. This awakening stems first from public opinion, and from the governments, but scientific and intellectual concepts have also played a part. We should remember that it was in Latin America that the ecosystem concept was first developed. It was as a result of the Stockholm meeting and of subsequent actions on the part of the United Nations Environmental Programme (UNEP), the Economic Commission for Latin America and the Caribbean (ECLAC), and other institutions concerned with the issue, that the concept of sustainable development within a particular ecosystem began to evolve. This concept also represents an intellectual progression. We are still at a stage where we can single out certain specific elements.

The first element is that in the interaction between man and nature, nature will clearly suffer some aggression. Some of this is inevitable and forms part of the appropriate use of natural resources to sustain economic and social development. However, it is also clear that the sources of aggression against the environment are varied. In the case of the industrial countries, environmental degradation is basically the result of their level of wealth, which leads to reckless use of resources and the profligate use of energy with little thought for conservation. In the developing countries, the basic factor causing degradation of the environment is poverty. And it is poverty that aggravates the deterioration of the urban environment, that fuels the irrational and destructive occupation of the land and forests, that generates pollution of the waterways and that creates air pollution in large urban areas. It is very important to bear this in mind, because to the extent that we recognize that the problem is different in developed and developing countries, we will begin to grasp that international solidarity on the environment is based on recognition of the differing perceptions we have of the problem. Only if we are able to understand these perceptions will we be in a position to build bridges of understanding to enable us to approach the problem collectively.

The second element is that there are problems that have acquired global dimensions. The warming of the atmosphere is a matter of world-wide concern, and rightly so, if controversial scientific projections point to the potential existence of a major problem that would have drastic implications for the ecosystems of the planet. This forms part of legitimate worry expressed by the international community. We now also see concern about acid rain and air pollution, well familiar to our friends in the United States, Canada, and the European Community, where industrialization causes sometimes irreversible damage to natural resources.

Damaging the ecology

This damage is the result of, among other things, the accelerated industrialization process itself. Residents of Mexico City, Santiago, and São Paulo are familiar with air pollution. In those cities, urban congestion is causing dangerous health hazards. Other global problems are toxic wastes and the more than 70,000 chemicals now in use throughout the world that are degrading soil, polluting waterways, and harming nature. Of course, Latin America could not escape from these problems. One of the problems that is perhaps most closely affecting the ecology in Latin America is population growth.

The Latin American region has one of the highest demographic growth rates in the world. In the 1960s and 1970s, we had a growth rate of 2.9 per cent. It has now dropped to 2.2 per cent, although we are still one of the regions with the highest growth and with ever-higher urban concentrations.

Deforestation is a worrisome topic in a number of regions, particularly the Amazon. Central America's rain forests are also facing similar deforestation. In countries that are being severely deforested today, such as El Salvador, Costa Rica, Nicaragua and Honduras, virgin forests will survive only in national parks. The same is true of Haiti and other Caribbean countries.

We also have the problem of water pollution in all countries of the region; degradation of basins containing precious ecosystems that we must preserve; the problem of the pampas and the savannahs, which gives rise to concern today in several countries, including Argentina and Uruguay; and the problem of coastal resources in the Caribbean Islands and other areas connected with that precious ecosystem, on which the United Nations has already taken specific actions; pollution from the improper use of agrochemicals due to the rapid expansion of agriculture, especially agribusiness; the possible destruction of the biological diversity and the wealth of germ plasms in Latin America, which constitutes one of mankind's most valuable reserves, and which we must somehow protect and defend. Indigenous communities must also be protected, not only because of ethics and the rights of citizenship, but also because of the huge store of knowledge and experience they have accumulated in the management of ecosystems down through the centuries. This knowledge is important not only for them, but also for present and future communities that will need an in-depth understanding of these ecological resources.

Lessons to be drawn

What conclusions can we draw from these points, which demonstrate the experience that has been gained regionally and internationally? The first seems obvious—the entire world has a severe problem, and Latin America has a severe problem. We are all equally committed. There is no distinction between global or regional concerns here. These are the concerns of the world community, which is confronting a problem that must be dealt with.

Secondly, the relationship between development and the environment is crucial. We cannot deal with the problem of development in isolation. Nor can we isolate the environmental problem. The two are essentially integral parts of a whole, and the relationship between them is not simple. It is even more complex now that new factors—large populations and evolving technologies—are changing the nature of the problem. There are no easy, straightforward answers. Often, we are concerned by the simplistic way these topics are approached, by our enormous lack of knowledge about resource management, and by the difficulty of arriving at satisfactory solutions. One of the lessons of the last 20 years—and I say this from personal experience—is that there are no easy ways to tackle these problems and that we must take precautions against dangerous simplifications and distortions of public opinion.

The other lesson we learn from history is that preventive measures always cost less than curative or regenerative measures. That is the principle the developed countries learned after despoiling their environment during their development; they are now having to use their resources to remedy this vicious circle. The developing world cannot repeat that mistake. We cannot propose to the developing world that its alternative is to destroy nature to achieve development only to regenerate it. That is too costly and is neither acceptable to the public nor feasible, given the weak economies of our countries. Accordingly, anticipation and prevention are fundamental, because they are the most economical, most rational, and most acceptable way to handle the present dimensions of the problem.

There is not enough information about these issues, especially about what is being done. But there are positive developments taking place in Latin America. There are positive developments at the national level: many laws are being enacted; agencies, ministries and institutes are being established; and environmental issues are even being included in constitutions (for example, the constitution recently adopted by Brazil). There are also positive developments at the multilateral level. We know more now than we did 20 years ago, when we embarked on hydroelectric or urban projects, because we have learned by doing. We have surely committed errors in the past that we will not repeat. Today, we are better prepared to face environmental challenges.

Financial needs

The people who work at the government level are fully aware of the enormous financial scope of environmental measures, both preventive and curative. And they are also aware of the great difficulties arising from the crisis. Some say that today poverty is a major source of environmental degradation; I would say that the economic crisis that Latin America is currently experiencing is much more the culprit than poverty itself. The crisis stems from the cutbacks in government budgets. A country cannot be asked to cut funding for health, education and nutrition, but to maintain it for ecology. Funding is cut across the board. The economic crisis, closely linked to the debt issue, has been one of the most serious sources of the deepening of the ecological crisis in Latin America.

Conclusion

We are facing a universal problem that is now one of the greatest challenges to the international community. But, I believe that the great problem of the environment is, in the last analysis, a problem of the individual and of society. It is at the national level that solidarity must prevail and sensitivity must be translated into specific actions.

It is incumbent upon the countries themselves and the national communities to define these problems. This does not mean that sovereignty is the only consideration. Sovereignty is very important and we cannot overlook it, for it is sovereignty that gave us independence more than 150 years ago. Along with that sovereignty, however, there is the principle of solidarity, which has become prevalent in the world in the last few decades. The two principles are not incompatible. Formulas can readily be found that are compatible with national perceptions of the problem and at the same time increase national and international solidarity on this issue.

This all leads to the paramount need to generate confidence in the parties actively involved with this issue. This topic is too serious and complicated to be undermined by a lack of confidence. Confidence is needed between the governments, the representatives of society, and institutions at the international level. The problem of the environment cannot be addressed through sanctions. It has to be based on a policy of cooperation. This is the only factor which, in the long run, can transform this problem into an enormous cooperative effort, a historic example of the generosity of present generations to future generations. This can be achieved only if we build bridges of confidence.

Chapter 5

PROMOTING ENVIRONMENTALLY SOUND ECONOMIC PROGRESS: WHAT THE NORTH CAN DO

Robert Repetto*

Can the world economy continue to expand without environmental repercussions that increasingly undermine living standards? The question is unavoidable because all economic activity depends on natural resources and inherently limited biological and chemical processes. Biological productivity and living organisms' resistance to climatic variations and other stresses are limited. The capacities of air, water, and soils to assimilate wastes are also limited. Overstepping these limits alters natural systems.

Since World War II, population has more than doubled and world economic activity has expanded roughly fivefold. Extensive environmental changes have resulted. In industrial countries, emissions have concentrated in the atmosphere, in surface and underground waters, and in land-based disposal sites. In developing countries, along with urban pollution, agricultural expansion and tree felling far beyond regeneration rates have greatly reduced natural forest cover and increased soil erosion.

*Director of the Program in Economics and Institutions, World Resource Institute, Washington D.C. The article is reprinted by kind permission of the World Resources Institute.

I
ECOLOGY AND
THE GLOBAL ECONOMY

Environmental impacts have become global. Greenhouse gases, such as carbon dioxide, methane, and chlorofluorocarbons, are building up in the atmosphere. Fossil fuel combustion and deforestation have increased carbon dioxide emissions to levels substantially above natural rates of withdrawal. Higher carbon dioxide concentrations in the air affect the heat balance of the earth and, consequently, surface temperatures, ocean and air currents, precipitation, and evaporation. Emissions of greenhouse gases can affect climate continents away and generations into the future. These effects are complex and not well understood, but they are highly non-linear and irreversible and may be compounded or mitigated by second- and third-order repercussions. Other environmental changes of global scope include the accelerating loss of genetic diversity due to tropical deforestation and loss of other species-rich habitats, the pollution of oceans, and the depletion of stratospheric ozone.

Such changes in natural systems have profound economic significance. Direct economic losses are suffered when supplies of minerals, forest products, and other natural resources commodities are depleted. Renewable resources, such as forest, also yield valuable economic services—water and soil retention, for example. Losing them raises economic costs associated with flooding, sedimentation, and the like. The "service" that greenhouse gases provide in mitigating temperature extremes are so substantial that should concentrations rise or fall beyond a limited range, human life on earth would be impossible.

Less obviously, natural systems provide demonstrably large economic benefits in themselves by enhancing the quality of life, although such values are not captured in standard economic accounts. One is not used to thinking of a favourable climate as an economic good, although people will incur substantial migration costs and accept lower monetary earnings to live in well-endowed regions. Adverse climate changes would impose direct economic losses by reducing the quality of life, as well as extra outlays on heating and cooling to mitigate the loss, and a variety of other effects on productivity.

Because of these economic losses, it is a serious concern that, as economic activity depletes natural resources and disturbs natural systems, net economic welfare might fall. Those who use up the resources might benefit, but at the expense of others who suffer the environmental impacts and of future generations for whom the resources and their services would be unavailable. Current economic welfare would then be obtained at the expense of future reductions in living standards.

The challenge of sustainable economic progress is leaving natural resources and systems sufficiently intact to permit continuing gains in economic welfare into the foreseeable future. In this spirit, the Brundtland Commission's definition of sustainability is development that "meets the needs of the present without compromising the ability of the future to meet its own needs".

Whether sustainable progress is possible globally is by no means obvious. Four decades of post-World War II economic development have left at least a billion people in dire poverty and most of the developing and the socialist countries in economic difficulty. It has created enormous economic difficulty. It has created enormous economic disparities between rich and poor (such that the average American uses as much energy as 20 Indians) without abating in the slightest the pressure for further economic growth in the most affluent countries. These currently receive net resource outflows form the less developed of $50 billion per year—the amount of Egypt's total gross national product. Arrested economic development has delayed the demographic transition so much that demographers now project world population ultimately stabilizing at 12 to 14 billion. Minimal forecasts of economic expansion likely to occur over the next 50 years imply a further fivefold expansion of the world's economy.

In view of the disruptions already occurring in natural systems, such an attempted expansion, absent a markedly different mode of economic activity, will result in the substantial further accumulation of greenhouse gases, the deterioration of air and water quality over large regions, the accumulation of industrial and household wastes, the depletion of natural resource stocks, and the accelerated loss of biological diversity.

II
MAKING ECONOMIC ACCOUNTS REFLECT ENVIRONMENTAL REALITIES

The economic significance of natural resources is not adequately reflected in economic accounting systems. The non-marketed, unpriced services that natural resources provide are typically not valued, while the expenditures forced on society by the loss of those services are. As a result, resource degradation often appears to raise, rather than lower economic welfare. For example, should toxic substances leak from a landfill to pollute waters and soils, measured income does not fall, despite possibly severe degradation of natural resources. If the government spends millions to clean up the mess, income rises because such expenditures are regarded as purchases of final goods and services. But, if industry undertakes the clean-up, even if under court orders, the expenditures are treated as intermediate costs and leave income unchanged. Finally, if the site is not cleaned up and nearby households suffer medical expenses or must purchase costly bottled water, measure income again rises because household outlays are considered final consumption in the national accounts. Inevitably, decisions based on such one-sided accounts are biased against resource conservation.

To make matters worse, natural resources are not consistently treated in economic accounting systems as economic assets. Like other forms of capital, natural resources provide a flow of economic benefits over time. Nonetheless, activities that deplete or degrade them are represented as generating income, rather than as reducing wealth. A country could sell off its timber and minerals, erode its soils, pollute its aquifers, deplete its fisheries, and the national accounts would treat all the proceeds as current income. Mistaking a decline in wealth for a rise in income is a confusion likely to end in bankruptcy.

A widely accepted definition of income, fully consistent with the Brundtland Commission's concept of sustainable development, is the maximum amount that can be consumed in the current period without reducing potential future consumption. In both business and national accounting, a capital consumption allowance representing the depreciation of the capital stock during the year is subtracted from net revenues in calculating annual income. This depreciation allowance reflects the amount needed to keep the capital stock intact. But depreciation is narrowly applied only to buildings and equipment. Failing to allow for depreciation of natural resource stocks when they are depleted or degraded disguises the sacrifice of future consumption, overstates income and capital formation and justifies policies that waste natural resources in the name of economic growth.

An important operational step toward integrating ecology and economics is to measure economic progress properly. Current economic accounting systems, which were developed when natural resource limitations seemed less pressing, should be revised. Two changes are of high priority.

First, natural resources for which economic values can be established should be treated as tangible capital in economic accounting frameworks. Additions to stocks should be treated as capital formation while depletion and degradation should be treated as capital consumption.

Second, pollution control and other identifiable "defensive expenditures" undertaken to prevent the loss of environmental services should be treated not as final expenditures but as intermediate costs (i.e., the cost of generating a *given* level of goods and services) whether undertaken by government, households, or enterprises.

There is extensive academic research literature on these revisions, and several governments within the Organisation for Economic Cooperation and Development (OECD) are making statistical estimates. A few developing country governments also have initiated resource accounts. Such international organizations as the OECD, the United Nations Environment Programme (UNEP), and the World Bank have sponsored conferences and research.

The United Nations Statistical Commission has a key role to play since most markets economies follow the United Nations System of National Accounts (SNA). In the current round of revisions to the SNA, which take place only every twenty years and will be completed in 1991, the Commission considered such changes but has tentatively decided against changes in the core accounts. As an alternative, the United Nations Statistical Office is drafting methodological guidelines for national statistical offices that wish to construct satellite resource and environmental accounts to supplement the core of basic accounts.

Faster reform is warranted. Few national statistical offices actually have the manpower or money to work on satellite accounts. In those few that do, politicians and the public pay little attention to the results, focusing instead on the more familiar measures of gross national product (GNP) and national income. The economic accounts are the foundation of planning, analysis, evaluation, and decision making and therefore:

(a) The United Nations Statistical Commission should establish a work programme aimed at incorporating these resource and environmental accounting revisions into the core system of national accounts within three to five years;

(b) More member governments, especially within the OECD, should adopt such changes in their national accounts;

(c) The World Bank and other development agencies should increase their assistance to developing countries in initiating resource accounting.

No other change could so powerfully demonstrate that steps to protect the environment are in countries' own economic interests.

III
INTEGRATING ENVIRONMENTAL
AND ECONOMIC OBJECTIVES

Promoting environmental productivity

Most post-war economic growth has resulted not from capital and labour accumulation, but from improvements in the quality of inputs and the efficiency with which they have been used. Productivity gains have been driven by vigorous innovation and rapid diffusion. However, productivity measures should include not just output per worker and per unit of capital. Output per unit of natural resources used and per unit of wastes discharged are important, neglected dimensions of productivity. The rate of improvement in this environmental dimension of productivity largely determines whether economic growth can be sustained without ecological damage. Governments should devote the same attention to "environmental" productivity as to conventional indicators of economic efficiency.

Technical innovation—energy-saving processes, for example— might raise both environmental and capital productivity. However, there could also be trade-offs. Should firms save capital by not installing pollution control equipment, the apparent gain in capital efficiency, at the expense of heavier environmental damage, could mask overall productivity losses.

Such trade-offs are probably important. Profit-oriented private decisions largely determine the direction of technological change. Although government research and development policies play a role, market incentives dominate the search for and adoption of new technologies. Since waste discharges are usually free, except for regulatory limits, there are few market incentives to seek and adopt waste-reducing technologies unless environmental efficiency gains are incidental to other cost savings, such as reduced raw material costs. On the contrary, there are considerable incentives to reduce costs at the expense of greater environmental damages not borne by the polluter.

Compounding the effect, government market interventions often artificially reduce the costs of natural resource commodities to users or raise the profits of suppliers. These interventions reduce incentives to adopt resource-saving technologies and increase environmental impacts from primarily commodity production. Examples are obvious: many governments heavily subsidize irrigation water, destroying farmers' incentives to adopt even simple and highly economic technologies to conserve water. Overall water-use efficiency is drastically reduced, and rivers, wetlands, groundwater, and soils also suffer significant loss of productivity, although few such losses impinge directly on the individual farmer. Resource subsidies create perverse incentives.

Reducing "policy failures" in government policies towards natural resource commodity markets is important in both industrial and developing countries, whether capitalist or socialist. Tax, credit, pricing, and other government policies towards natural resource industries often discourage resource conservation while reducing economic productivity, increasing fiscal burdens on government, and reinforcing inequities. Energy, water, forest, industrial, and agricultural sectors are all greatly affected by these interventions. Producer incentives are often biased towards depletion or degradation of the resource base and potentially more efficient production systems are discouraged.

Economic instruments can also correct incentives by making waste generators pay the economic costs of disrupting natural systems. Emissions charges, marketable emissions permits, non-compliance charges linked to emissions standards, deposit and return systems, and assignment of legal liability for pollution damages are among the policies that can discourage pollution. They decentralize technological choices about environmental protection with the enterprise manager, who generally knows best which technologies fit and perform well in his situation, and confront managers with the full incremental costs both of abating and of not abating their emissions. For these reasons, economic instruments are generally more effective in promoting appropriate technological innovation then "command-and-control" regulations and the former lead to more efficient environmental control.

These economic instruments have performed as expected when tried. Yet, few governments have used economic instruments to deal with "market failures" to the extent the potential warrants. The costs of disturbing natural systems must be incorporated much more systematically into the profit-loss calculus of enterprises and households if environmental productivity is to rise sufficiently to permit sustainable development.

Promoting concern for the future

At long-term interest rates of about 10 per cent, an ecological loss of a million dollars expected to happen in a hundred years has a present cost of $75. For consumers borrowing at 18 per cent per year on their credit cards, it would have a present cost of $0.06. The implication, obviously irrational, is that global climate change or loss of biological diversity, which risk potentially enormous losses over the next century, can be virtually ignored in current government and private decisions that will significantly affect those future developments.

Future costs and benefits, if discounted at all in public investment decisions, should reflect society's valuation of future welfare. Nonetheless, many national governmental and inter-governmental agencies continue to use private market interest rates for investment analysis. The World Bank and the International Development Association (IDA), for example, screen projects with a 10 per cent rate of return. The Inter-American Development Bank (IDB) uses a 12 per cent discount rate. Instead, project benefits and costs should be evaluated using a much lower risk and inflation-free discount rate—say, 2 per cent—and investments should then be screened by requiring a high ratio of discounted benefits to (discounted) costs. Many scientists would argue that even a 2 per cent discount rate, which implies that costs incurred 35 years in the future are only half as important as those incurred now, is too myopic, but a 2 per cent rate puts 1900 times more weight on consequences a hundred years hence than does a 10 per cent rate.

Public and international agencies, including particularly the multilateral development banks, should be directed by their governing bodies to adopt this alternative approach to investment evaluation.

Public policy can manifest concern for future welfare most powerfully by encouraging greater private savings and investment. High private-market interest rates reflect heavy competition among public and private borrowers for limited savings. United States fiscal policy, perhaps more than that of most industrial countries, penalizes savings and rewards borrowing. Taxation of personal dividend income as well as that of corporate profits, capital gains, and legacies effectively subject savings to multiple taxation. Simultaneously, business and personal borrowing costs are lowered by the deductibility of most interest payments from taxable income. This fiscal orientation, together with heavy public borrowing, pushes market interest rates up and shortens economic time horizons.

IV
STEPS TOWARD INTEGRATING ECONOMICS AND ECOLOGY

Public forests

Forests are under heavy but varied pressures throughout the world. In industrial regions, forests are threatened by local and kong-range air pollution. In the United States and some other affluent countries, public forests face severe problems in managing conflicting demands for the services and commodities they provide. In most developing countries, forests are being rapidly depleted and converted to other land uses, with grave economic and ecological losses.

Industrialized countries

Forestry traditions in most of Europe ensure that public forests are husbanded for the multiple benefits they provide, but forestry practice in more sparsely settled areas of the United States, Canada, and

Australia gives effective pre-eminence to timber production. These priorities often conflict with the increasingly important recreational and ecological benefits that forests provide.

Such biases can be corrected by managing public forests more economically. Budgetary subsidies for timber production should be eliminated, except for appropriations to protect biological diversity and other non-marketable services. Forest road construction and management should be financed out of net revenues. User fees based on market values or the willingness of the consumer to pay should be collected for non-timber commodity production (including mining rights), livestock grazing rights, recreational uses, and other services from public forests—thus establishing the value of other forest benefits. Such measures to ensure that governments obtain fair market value for commodities and services produced in public forests and to reduce government subsidies for resource exploitation on public lands will encourage more sustainable forest management in several temperate zone countries.

Tropical countries

Tropical forests are being rapidly and wastefully depleted. Inappropriate and unsustainable exploitation is dissipating much of the forest wealth of most tropical countries. Governments are realizing little of the potential benefits. Rationalizing forest management, collecting fair market value for timber, and reducing subsidies for competing agricultural uses can greatly reduce the wastage. Tropical deforestation, which threatens biological diversity and the earth's climate, is a global concern and should be addressed through international cooperation.

European countries, the United States and Japan are the main markets for tropical timber exports, and their multinational companies are deeply involved in tropical timber exploitation. Governments of all importing countries should ensure that these companies, their subsidiaries, and their affiliates strictly adhere to all host-country laws and regulations regarding timber operations, export restrictions, and tax and royalty payments. In addition, importing countries should support and strengthen the role of the International Tropical Timber

Organization in monitoring compliance, publicizing violations,and negotiating remedies.

The Tropical Forest Action Plan (TFAP) is an international effort to identify and fund high-priority actions to strengthen forestry management, research, conservation, and policy affecting tropical forests. With a secretariat located in the Food and Agriculture Organization of the United Nations, participation from all interested constituencies, and national plans under way in more than fifty countries, it is a vehicle for international cooperation. Industrialized countries should provide financial and technical support for both planning implementation. Sponsors should ensure that the TFAP generates higher long-term returns to tropical countries by designing forest revenue systems that promote sustained yield management and collect fair market value for tropical timber and non-timber products.

The multilateral development banks are now formulating forest-sector loans that address the need to improve forest-revenue policies, to strengthen institutions, and to meet other concerns, Member countries should support these activities in the governing bodies of the banks and through co-financing.

As part of the TFAP and other development cooperation programmes in forestry, investments in reforestation should be markedly increased, In most countries, the private sector has a better record in plantation and community forestry than does the government, but because forestry is a long-term investment, private participation depends on security of tenure and predictable policies. Development agencies and host governments in developing countries should cooperate in expanding reforestation, community forestry, and plantation programmes.

Managing long-range air pollution damage

Throughout most of Europe and North America, airborne emissions of sulphur and nitrogen oxide, reacting with volatile organic compounds and drifting over long distances, are acidifying forests and aquatic ecosystems, and causing other damage. Considerable research into emissions sources, atmospheric transport and chemistry, and ecological responses has justified public concern. Governments have tightened emissions standards on both mobile and stationary pollution sources, but actions have been limited by the high costs of emissions reductions from coal-fired power plants, vehicles, and industrial furnaces. Decisions have also been complicated because much of the pollution drifts across jurisdictional boundaries. Jurisdictions exporting pollution gain only part of the benefits from clean-up, while those importing pollution have no authority over damaging source.

Governments in Europe and America have recognized that precursor emissions should be reduced by international agreement and are negotiating the difficult issue of responsibilities for abatement in different jurisdictions. Economic studies show that the costs of achieving any predetermined overall abatement level can be greatly reduced if policies allow flexibility as to where and how abatement should take place and avoid prescribing either specific technologies, such as flue gas desulphurization, or rigid allocations of emissions reduction among source.

Innovative regulatory instruments such as the "bubble" and "marketable emissions reduction credits" can provide this flexibility. A bubble is an overall emissions reduction target for a group of sources that allows them discretion on how best to achieve it. The bubble concept has recently been applied in United States legislative proposals on acid rain: overall sulphur-abatement targets were set for each state but how those targets should be met was not specified. This policy allows each state to concentrate on low-cost sources and means of abatement.

Marketable emissions-reduction credits that are transferable across jurisdictional boundaries are an innovative economic instrument that could further strengthen long-range pollution control. In operation, each source would be allowed to transfer all or part of its permitted emissions to another agency for monetary compensation. Sources that would incur high abatement costs could compensate low-cost sources in other jurisdictions for cutting back further than otherwise required. Differences among jurisdictions tend to narrow. Moreover, should some jurisdictions experience exceptionally high damages from pollution orig-inating elsewhere,they could compensate sources in the offending re-gion for cutting back more than in minimal prescribed amount.

Intergovernmental institutional cooperation is essential to realize these benefits. A mechanism to record and enforce these transfers across jurisdictional boundaries would have to be created. In Europe, the European Economic Community (EEC) might consider this inno-vation. In the United States, the Environmental Protection Agency (EPA) should authorized to operate such a mechanism in tandem with its emissions trading programme and to open discussions with its Canadian counterpart on international transferability.

Water

In most regions, inland and coastal water quality is increasingly threat-ened by pollution. Regulations requiring large industrial and municipal sources to treat their wastes before discharging them need to be strength-ened in many countries. In dense urban and industrial areas, even the sheer volume of treated discharges can degrade water quality. More-over, few countries effectively control "non-point source" effluents from agriculture, construction, and transport. These effluents—a large, rap-idly growing source of water pollution—include discharges to air and soils that finally find their way into water bodies. Regulations requiring wastewater treatment by large sources cannot combat these broader problems.

Semi-arid areas, such as the American West, also face increasing competition for water. Agriculture has long used most of the available water, disturbing rivers and wetlands. Good dam sites have been occu-pied, underground aquifers depleted, and municipal and recreational uses have increased, so the costs of supplying agricultural demands have risen sharply. Fertilizers, pesticide residues, and salts washed from irri-gated fields have created increasingly intractable environmental prob-lems. Yet, highly subsidized public water supplies, the weakness of institutional mechanism for transferring water among potential users, and the lack of regulatory control over agricultural effluents and return flows have insulated farmers from these rising problems. To safeguard this vital resource, governments must resolve to treat water as a valuable economic resource and impose its full costs on those who use or degrade it.

Water pricing

In most countries, urban and rural water charges are far below incremental supply costs. Flat rate fees unrelated to use, average cost-pricing, and declining block tariffs are widely employed. They are inferior to marginal cost-pricing structures combining incremental capital costs and volumetric charges covering operating costs. Volumetric charges should incorporate drainage costs for irrigation waters and sewage costs for household users. Industrial users, most of whom can control the volume and content of water-borne discharges by making technical modifications, should face sewage and wastewater treatment charges based on the incremental costs of treating discharges with specific characteristics and volumes.

Marginal cost-pricing encourages water conservation and thereby reduces the need for new storage and diversions while providing financial resources for maintenance and improvements. At the same time, pollution from contaminated return flows diminishes. Wastewater treatment and drainage charges also encourage enterprises to control and prevent discharges on site through relatively efficient process modifications.

Adopting marginal cost water-pricing approaches may require worthwhile investments in metering, and the move certainly faces political resistance, especially from highly subsidized users. Nonetheless, pricing that incorporates full supply and environmental costs is the strongest instrument available to encourage efficient water use, promote the adoption of less polluting technologies, and conserve increasingly scarce water resources.

By financing highly subsidized water projects and failing to insist on pricing approaches that encourage efficiency in water use, bilateral and multilateral development assistance agencies contribute to these wasteful approaches in developing countries as well.

The result is gross inefficiency in water use in most developing countries, overinvestment in new construction at the expense of the maintenance of existing systems, and serious ecological damage to soils and river basins. Although food security and poverty alleviation are advanced to justify the situation, the principal beneficiaries are better-off landowners and urban middle classes. Imposing economically realistic user-charges is virtually the only way to put a stop to the pervasive pork-barrel politics of water-project investments.Member governments should ensure that bilateral and multilateral development assistance agencies adopt and enforce in water projects the same principles of financial autonomy cost recovery and marginal cost pricing that are applied to other public utilities.

Several European governments have also used pricing mechanisms in the control of water pollution by levying fees or charges on emissions. Other governments should emulate the European response. For the most part, however, charges have been revenue devices ancillary to administrative emissions control and the rates have been too low relative to treatment costs to limit the discharge of wastes to the assimilative capacity of water bodies. Higher rates and less reliance on technology-based emissions standards would encourage further abatement and efficient process changes.

Water transfers

Governments should also provide greater scope for voluntary transfers of rights to use water, either as a production input or as a receptacle for wastes. In the United States, limited sales and lease markets for water transfers among irrigation users, and between rural and urban users, have emerged despite high transaction costs and considerable uncertainty over property rights to in-stream and return flows. Instituting explicit legal mechanisms for establishing and transferring such rights and protecting the interests of third parties would encourage these transactions, which reallocate water to more valuable users. Issuing shares in public irrigation projects that would entitle shareholders to a proportionate fraction of available water each year and allowing leases and sales of such shares is such an institutional mechanism.

Governments that have not yet done so should adjudicate the rights of corporate and individual claimants to groundwater. Clarifying these rights would strengthen private incentives to conserve groundwater and enable interested parties to seek compensation for damages from contamination. In countries where rights over groundwater will remain vested in governments, charges for withdrawal and penalties for contamination can still bolster administrative regulations.

Controlling non-point source emissions

This growing problem can be addressed not by traditional source-by-source regulation, but only through more far-reaching policies, including the use of economic incentives. In agriculture, for example, overuse or inefficient application of fertilizers, pesticides, and irrigation water, and intensive cultivation of erodible soils adjoining water bodies have resulted in serious pollution of surface and underground water in many areas. In the Netherlands, nearly 25 per cent of groundwater supplies contain nitrates in concentrations hazardous to health and 20 per cent of acid depositions has been traced to ammonia released by farm operations. Higher prices for chemical and water inputs, whether through fees or reduced subsidies, can induce more efficient use and encourage the diffusion of agricultural technologies that are less input-intensive. Several ECE countries have already imposed charges on farm chemicals to discourage excessive use and finance environmental programmes, in accordance with the "polluter pay" principle.

More fundamental changes in farm-support policies in European countries, the United States, and Japan would reduce non-point source pollution from agriculture even more powerfully. At present, measures that raise farmers' income by supporting agricultural commodity prices induce farmers to apply chemical and other inputs more heavily to their cultivated acreage. Despite acreage limitations built into some agricultural support programmes to control production surpluses, the net effect of price supports is to raise total input use. Regulations such as "cross-compliance" provisions in United States agricultural policy are designed to mitigate these environmental effects by discouraging the cultivation of highly erodible soils. In addition, specific regulations on pesticide use and the protection of drinking-water supplies seek to balance agricultural benefits against health risks. However, such regulations cannot reverse the strong overall incentives farm-support programmes create to intensify chemical use. Providing targeted farm-income supplements and subsidies more directly, instead of manipulating farm prices, would lead to less intensive cultivation and less agricultural pollution.

Promoting sustainable agriculture

The agricultural sector has recorded remarkable gains in output and yields. Yet, it suffers from serious economic and ecological distortions that may prove unsustainable. In advanced regions, output gains have been achieved at the cost of heavy and rising energy inputs, both mechanical and chemical, which make the agricultural sector quite vulnerable to rising energy costs. Farmers in many irrigated areas are squeezed between rising real supply costs for water and rising environmental costs due to soil salinization and drainage problems. Intensive cultivation has raised erosion rates in some regions to levels that imply serious soil fertility losses and even larger off-site sedimentation costs. Despite doubled and redoubled pesticide applications, the fraction of many crops lost to pest has not declined, and the number of pests resistant to one or more chemicals has risen sharply. Financially, the farm sector has become increasingly dependent on government support. These trends are potentially unsustainable.

Agriculture is also a major contributor to off-farm environmental problems. In the United States, for example, 70 per cent of nutrients and 33 per cent of sediments reaching waterways come from agricultural land. Twenty per cent of the nation's wells are contaminated by nitrates from fertilizers, and in the Iowa cornbelt, where three out of four people drink well water, 40 per cent of tested wells show pesticide contamination and 40 per cent exceed EPA maximum health limits for nitrates. In the agricultural areas of Western Europe, the same problems of water pollution, soil erosion, and exceedingly heavy input use have been documented.

Agricultural policy in the United States, the European Community, and Japan exacerbates these environmental problems. Supporting farm incomes through import restrictions and export subsidies, through direct price supports and supplemental payments linked to historical production levels, and through input subsidies induces farmers to expand the acreage of crops under support programmes and to use more inputs on those crops.

Import restrictions on sugar, dairy products, and other agricultural products raise domestic prices and thus increase both acreage and inputs used in protected regions. These restrictions involve economic losses to consumers and more efficient producers (located mainly in less developed countries) and increase pollution problems. Direct price supports also expand acreage and input use, with similar economic and environmental costs, but also large fiscal costs, if supported by government stockpiles or export subsides. Price support programmes have typically needed acreage limitations to reduce surpluses, but farmers respond by retiring their least productive land (not necessarily the land most prone to environmental damage) and using even more inputs on the rest. The environmental benefits of acreage limitations can be increased by targeting cutbacks on sensitive ares, including stream borders and groundwater-recharge zones.

In the United States, supplemental "deficiency" payments increase the net receipts of producers of cotton, wheat, corn, sorghum, and rice. Payments represent the difference between target and market (or floor) prices multiplied by historical production levels. These levels are calculated as past average acreages and yields. Such supplemental payments keep more acreage in relatively erosive, chemical-intensive programme crops. They also discourage crop rotations involving non-programme crops, such as leguminous cover crops because they reduce "base acreage" and potential future support payments. Since crop rotations are fundamental to low-input regenerative farming systems, this policy promotes intensive monocultures.

Governments have tried to reduce these environmental damages by additional interventions, such as "cross-compliance" provisions regulating the farming of vulnerable soils or inappropriate input use. In addition, land-retirement schemes, such as the United States Conservation Reserve Program, have been targeted toward soil conservation. These are stop-gap, mitigating measures, however, and do not obviate the pressing need, on both economic and environmental grounds, for more fundamental change. Farm policy in the United States, Japan, and Western Europe has been economically inefficient, raising producers' income at a much larger cost to consumers and taxpayers, exceedingly burdensome fiscally, disruptive of trading relations among these regions, harmful to agricultural producers in other regions, particularly in developing countries, and highly regressive (since benefits are proportional to the amounts produced). In addition, these policies encourage environmentally damaging and ecologically unsustainable farming systems.

These countries should move swiftly to alternative agricultural policies based on direct income support for targeted producers and practices and dismantle interventions that support farm prices and distort production decisions. "Decoupling" support programmes from market interventions in this way would greatly reduce the fiscal costs of agricultural policy and allow governments to target subsidies much more accurately on worthwhile policy objectives. Decoupling would also greatly reduce the economic costs of agricultural policies by allowing undistorted market incentives to reallocate crop production to regions and nations with comparative advantage while inducing farmers to make efficient profit-maximizing choices among alternative technologies. It would greatly reduce environmental damage from agricultural production by eliminating policy-induced incentives for excessively intensive acreage cultivation and input use and by encouraging sustainable and regenerative cropping systems.

Undoing fifty years of market intervention will necessitate considerable structural adjustment in agriculture—a painful process that many politicians, farmers, and agribusinesses are unwilling to undertake. But gains will greatly outweigh losses. Ironically, the structural adjustments that the industrial countries are calling on developing and socialist countries to make are much more extensive, and those countries have far fewer resources with which to cushion the process. The present value of future fiscal and economic savings from eliminating agricultural distortions would provide ample resources with which to finance an agricultural structural adjustment programme. This four-part programme would eliminate all market interventions, replace them with direct-income supports subject to reasonable ceilings and phasing-down over several years, refinance facilities to deal with changes in land and other agricultural asset values, and provide temporary financial assistance to cushion agribusiness dislocations.

V
ECONOMIC POLICIES TO PROMOTE POLLUTION PREVENTION

Pollution prevention or pollution control

Environmental policies in all countries have emphasized pollution control i.e., treating emissions to reduce their environmental impact rather than pollution prevention i.e., reducing the amount of waste produced. But the latter has many advantages:

- Controlling pollution in one medium often merely transfers wastes to another medium, at considerable cost and sometimes little environmental gain;

- Designing waste reducing processes into industrial plants is often much cheaper than controlling pollution through end-of-pipe techniques or cleaning up degraded environments; and

- Producing less waste also saves costly raw materials, a double bonus.

Many governments have established programmes such as sponsored research and information exchanges to encourage the adoption of low-waste technologies. These programmes are useful only if enterprises receive strong incentives to seek ways to reduce emissions and wastage of materials and energy. Economic instruments can help create those incentives.

Ideally, pollution could be efficiently prevented by comprehensive emission charges or transferable emission permits, which would put the correct environmental price on all wastes going to air, water, or land. For the enterprise, a large waste stream would inevitably result in heavy costs. Firms would respond according to their circumstances: some would install cleaner technologies now, others later, when equipment is replaced. Some would recycle more wastes into other processes, others would modify their products. These flexible, incentive-driven responses would achieve environmental quality standards at the lowest possible cost and promote technical innovations.

Unfortunately, in the real world, ideal economic instruments are impossible, partly because it is costly for regulators to get information about abatement costs and emissions damages in various media. Environmental and health damages might not come to light for years, for example. Information for enforcement is also hard to obtain: illegal disposal or discharge is often difficult to detect. Charges imposed on emissions at rates related to the marginal damages they cause might encourage "midnight dumping", or concentrate emissions in less strictly regulated media.

Ideal policies also ignore the political reality that heavy charges may put disruptive financial burdens on industry and increase the risk of rising local unemployment. Realistic pollution prevention policies must, like ideal instruments, create incentives for flexible, efficient responses and innovations to prevent pollution in many different circumstances, but take account of information costs and political realities.

Governments should move toward controlling emissions in all media with economic instruments. Emissions charges can be made more palatable by refunding some of the revenues to the industry as subsidies for technological innovation, or by exempting small amounts of emissions from the charge. Transferable emissions permits can also be granted free to existing emission sources instead of being auctioned off or sold. These modifications reduce the financial burden on industrial sources while retaining the same incentive effects at the margin.

Other economic instruments that take account of information and enforcement costs may be more feasible in some circumstances. For example, making emitters clearly liable for any damages they cause, with the burden of proof on the industry to establish harmlessness unless the emission level falls within established safety standards, has proven effective in obtaining industry's cooperation in standard-setting. By contrast, when the burden of proof is on the victim to establish that emissions above a standard have caused harm, industries have frequently resisted standard setting.

Economic instruments applied to process inputs rather than to waste outputs are especially relevant if wastes are hard to monitor and there is a fixed relation between inputs and wastes. Thus, a tax on the carbon content of fuels purchased will work better than a tax on carbon dioxide emissions. Even if the input is incorporated into the product, like cadmium in batteries, an input tax may be appropriate if eventual product disposal will cause problems.

Deposit-refund systems may be appropriate if monitoring discharges is difficult, as it is with many hazardous wastes. Deposit-refund systems not only discourage the discharge of waste, but also encourage sources to dispose of it properly. Such systems work by taxing some industrial input or consumer product (such as beverage containers or cars) and granting a refund when an approved method of disposal or recycling is followed. Deposit-refund systems have been successful (in the form of "bottle bills", for example), and governments of Northern nations should apply them more widely.

Raw material prices play an important part in preventing pollution. If prices are "too low", there is little incentive to use less raw material per unit of output and, because raw materials are not destroyed in the production process but only transformed, the excess inputs will end up as increased wastes. Also, low raw material prices undercut the demand for recycled inputs. Raw material prices must at the very least reflect the full private costs of extraction, so as to avoid an unjustified bias in favour of virgin instead of recycled (and, hence, waste-reducing) materials. Governments should examine their tax and tariff codes with a mind to eliminating allowances that reduce prices of virgin materials and remove other implicit subsidies to virgin materials users. Furthermore, taxes on virgin materials coupled to rebates to purchasers for the use of recycled materials are analogous to deposit-return systems and can help provide broader markets for recycled materials.

When regulatory rather than economic instruments are the prime method of pollution prevention, enforcement is handicapped because in many Northern countries fines for violations are so low that it pays polluters handsomely to break the law. To avoid time-consuming litigation, it is better to use non-compliance fees rather than criminal prosecution, provided that these fees are set so that firms have a strong incentive to abode by the regulations. Non-compliance penalties should be related to the extent and duration of the violation, and exceed the source's estimated costs of compliance.

Energy

Energy is essential for every industrial and commercial process and cannot be recycled. Because the supply of fossil fuels is finite and non-renewable, future generations may not have the same access to cheap energy sources that we do. Moreover, extracting, transporting, and converting all forms of energy imposes environmental costs, although some energy forms are less damaging than others. For these reasons, ecologically sound development must include policies that achieve a sustainable energy system and take the environmental costs of energy use fully into account.

Promoting energy efficiency and sustainability

Promoting energy efficiency is the least costly and most effective immediate option for reducing the local, regional, and global environmental problems associated with energy use. In all countries, and particularly in developing countries, the scope for economically and technically feasible investments in energy efficiency is large. Grasping these opportunities offers attractive returns over expanding energy supplies and can save many tens of billions of investment dollars over the next decade. Promoting energy efficiency requires governments to reduce energy subsidies. Governments in most countries are deeply involved in energy markets, through public ownership, regulation, and fiscal interventions. As a result, while some energy sources and uses are heavily taxed, others are available to users at far less than the incremental costs of supply, which includes environmental side effects. Government ownership or regulation of some energy supplies, although theoretically justified by economies of scale in conversion or distribution, has usually been a vehicle for direct and indirect energy subsidies. The belief that cheap energy is essential for economic growth is behind energy subsidies, but low energy prices typically mean low and stagnant energy efficiency, not rapid economic growth. On the contrary, many countries have achieved rapid economic growth since 1973 with relatively high energy prices and little increase in energy consumption.

Given this constellation of factors, all governments should seek to eliminate unwarranted subsidies in energy industries, whether direct or indirect. At a minimum, energy prices should reflect full incremental supply costs, including the costs of adequate environmental controls. Coal industries, in particular, are subsidized in many countries, despite coal's high environmental costs. Using public funds to cushion the redeployment of coalminers would be economically and ecologically preferable. Nuclear power has also been heavily subsidized in many countries. If nuclear power stations were transferred from the public to the private sector and hidden subsidies removed, electricity rates would better reflect real supply costs, encouraging energy conservation. Such changes are particularly likely to raise energy efficiency in Eastern European economies, where prices are well below world levels, and energy use per unit of gross domestic product (GDP) is roughly twice as high as in Western Europe.

The regulated monopolies and public ownership typical in the electricity-generation industry constitute barriers to efficient investment and energy use. Electric utilities should be reoriented to become profit-seeking vendors of energy services, not mere suppliers of kilowatt hours. To accomplish this, the link between electricity output and utility earnings must be broken. Generating companies must be able to profit by reducing sales, so long as costs fall faster than revenues. To these ends:

- Governments should ensure that cogenerators and independent electricity generators have a fair chance to compete with large centrally owned power stations, by inducing power companies to accept all competitive supply offers and to ensure independent suppliers access to transmission and distribution grids;

- Regulations should also create appropriate incentives for power companies to accept "demand side" bids from suppliers of electricity conservation and to supply energy efficiency services themselves. Electricity rate regulations should allow suppliers to retain profits from efficiency gains and investments in energy efficiency;

- Tariff policies should replace average cost-pricing and declining block rates with economically rational marginal cost pricing systems.

If these incentives are put in place, very extensive investments in energy efficiency will be possible at high rates of return.

Enormous savings are also possible in developing and previously centrally planned economies. It would be a costly mistake for these countries to equate development with a quantitative expansion of energy supplies, ignoring highly profitable opportunities to adopt energy efficient technologies and systems in making new investments. International investment banks, particularly the multilateral development banks, should be instructed by their directors to significantly increase the focus on energy efficiency in their new lending to developing countries and to Eastern Europe. Since many energy efficiency programmes require interventions that are dispersed and relatively small-scale, institution-building and expanding private sector participation are essential to success.

Consumers make most choices about energy use indirectly when buying cars, houses, and appliances. Unless consumers are fully informed about the energy efficiency of such durable purchases, they are likely to be cheaper but less efficient ones. Information may not suffice if incentives are lacking, as is the case when the owner of commercial real estate has no incentive to invest in energy conservation because he or she does not pay the energy bills. Incentives are also weak if industries have "soft budget constraints" and can simply pass along higher energy costs to customers or to government financing agencies. Policies to promote energy efficiency must permit market forces to function effectively by ensuring that people have enough information to make wise choices on energy use and by creating appropriate incentives. To these ends:

- Much more rigorous "energy labelling" of refrigerators, washing machines, domestic furnaces, the insulation and structure of houses, and vehicles is clearly needed;

- Industrial standards and building codes should be revised to promote greater energy efficiency;

- Legislation should ensure that energy service companies have the information and legal structure they need to realize the tremendous potential for profitable investments in energy efficiency in commercial and residential buildings. Mandatory energy labelling and metering of all new buildings and legal rights for tenants to hire energy service companies will help to achieve the potential for energy saving.

Transportation imposes environmental costs on the economy from air pollution, noise, congestion, and accidents. Predictions of dramatic traffic growth in many Northern countries over the next decade or two largely ignore these costs, and such growth may therefore be neither sustainable not desirable. Policies are needed to ensure that environmental costs are reflected in the prices that transport users pay. Substantial increases in gasoline and diesel taxes are warranted, especially in countries such as the United States and Canada, where they are now relatively low. This one change will simultaneously create pervasive but flexible incentives for more efficient engines, smaller cars, shorter journeys, better public transport, and (in the long term) less dispersed city layouts without impinging on personal freedom of travel.

Administrative controls on specific environmental impacts are also necessary. Vehicle emission standards should be enforced in all Northern countries. More traffic-free areas should be introduced in urban areas, and speed limits, which also affect safety, need to be enforced. But opportunities for economic incentives should be used wherever possible by:

- Relating vehicle taxes more closely to fuel consumption and environmental impacts;

- Introducing tolls and road-pricing schemes where practicable in congested city areas;

- Relating aircraft landing fees to noise and air pollution generated, and to the time of day; and

- Decoupling revenues from transportation and fuel taxes from public expenditures on particular transport modes (e.g., by abolishing the United States Interstate Highway Fund).

Environmental impacts of energy use

The environmental impacts of energy use are pervasive. Burning any fossil fuel releases carbon dioxide into the global atmosphere. Coal use also causes water pollution and subsidence or landscape scarring when it is mined, and particulate and sulphur dioxide pollution when it is burned. The lignite burned in many East European countries is particularly polluting. Petroleum extraction results in oil spills at sea. Attempts to "disperse and dilute" sulphur dioxide and other pollutants by building tall chimneys results in acid precipitation many hundreds of miles away. Gasoline use in automobile engines releases a variety of air pollutants—such as nitrogen oxide, carbon monoxide, and volatile organic compounds (VOCs)—that cause photochemical smog in urban areas. Natural gas (methane) is relatively free of impurities, and produces the lowest carbon dioxide per unit of heat of all fossil fuels, but is itself a powerful greenhouse gas. Leaks from natural gas wells and pipelines and the methane flared at large oilfields contribute to global warming.

Nuclear power, while not a greenhouse gas emitter, creates environmental problems from uranium mining wastes, accidents in operating nuclear plants, long-lived nuclear wastes, and the proliferation of nuclear weapons. For these reasons, it has suffered a dramatic loss of public confidence in most Northern countries. Renewable energy sources are inherently low density, so large areas of collectors (whether windmills, ware generators, tidal barrages, solar mirrors, solar cells, or biomass fuel plantations) are needed to collect energy in significant quantities. These inevitably affect the environment, both visually and ecologically.

Policies to control the environmental impacts of energy use in northern countries have concentrated largely on administrative or "command and control" methods, which usually impose very uneven control costs on users and so increase the total cost of achieving any abatement since total costs could be reduced by shifting more of the clean-up onto sources with low abatement costs. They also provide little incentive to industries to develop new and more efficient technologies for emissions control. EEC governments should therefore strive for greater efficiency in energy pollution control by steadily introducing economic instruments that reflect the environmental costs of energy use. Two well-known economic instruments are emissions charges and transferable emissions permits, but others, such as differential taxes on energy-using equipment (say, automobiles) may be appropriate.

The most important pollutants in the energy sector are sulphur dioxide, carbon dioxide, nitrogen oxide, and VOCs. Transferable emissions permits would lower the costs of achieving negotiated targets for reducing sulphur dioxide, VOCs, and nitrogen oxide emissions (see discussion of acid rain damage to forests), but they are potentially applicable to local as well as to transboundary pollution control programmes. "Bubble" policies can greatly reduce abatement costs for multi-source enterprises, while "off-sets" and other systems of transferable permits provide flexible, effective incentives for controlling conventional atmospheric emissions.

By contrast, carbon dioxide is a pollutant with many emissions sources, both large and small. Basing national or international control programmes on a system of quantitative permits would be administratively expensive and economically risky, for reasons discussed below. Individual national actions and international agreement to reduce carbon dioxide emissions are better supported by carbon taxes. An international agreement to stabilize the world climate should include coordinated national taxes on fossil fuels at rates proportionate to their carbon dioxide emissions per BTU and at levels designed to reduce overall global carbon dioxide emissions substantially.

Effective carbon taxes would produce considerable revenues. To avoid macroeconomic disruption, they would have to be phased in gradually and be partially offset by reductions in other taxes. But it would be possible to design a revenue package that would avoid the regressive impacts of energy taxes, offset some of the impacts of higher energy taxes on business costs, and maintain overall fiscal balance.

Promoting sustainable development internationally

Meeting the pressing needs of their increasing populations for better living standards without further depleting and degrading their natural environments is an urgent task for developing countries. Economic recovery is no less desperately needed in Eastern Europe. Moreover, it must be achieved predominantly by the efforts of these countries themselves through far-reaching changes in priorities and policies. What the developed market economies can and should provide is a more supportive policy framework for international trade, investment, and finance—one that will at least remove the severe impediments to sustainable development that less affluent countries now face.

Trade policies

International trade is still an engine of development. Despite pleas by trade pessimists and political utopians for self-sufficiency, countries must trade to gain access to technology, finance, and goods they cannot produce efficiently. However, countries without ample capital resources or advanced technology can profitably export only labour-intensive or natural resource-intensive products. Despite concern in the North about natural resources depletion in developing countries, the North's trade barriers strongly discourage developing countries from exporting more labour-intensive commodities. Facing such barriers, many developing countries rely on mineral and agricultural export industries, which draw heavily on natural resources.

Restrictions on market access, such as the Multi-Fibre Agreement and other quantitative restrictions, which apply most widely to labour-intensive manufacture from developing countries, constitute the most serious barrier since no comparative advantage can surmount them. These barriers are also expensive for the United States, Japan, and European countries that maintain them since every protected relatively low-productivity job costs several times its worth in higher costs to consumers. But, worse, barriers discourage developing countries from less environmentally burdensome labour-intensive manufacturing exports and contribute to unsustainable natural resource depletion. For these reasons, governments should quickly phase out quantitative import restrictions on labour-intensive manufacturers, using domestic policy measures to facilitate the necessary redeployment of labour and capital. If used at all, quantitative restrictions should be imposed to deny international markets access to products based on endangered species, tropical timber harvested in contravention of host country forestry regulations, and other ecologically hazardous exports.

Along the same lines, industrialized country trade policies protect their own processing industries and make it difficult for developing countries to increase the value added to raw materials prior to export. Almost invariably, industrialized country tariffs are substantially higher, the more highly processed the material. Thus, for example, if logs can be imported duty free, sawn timber would pay a tariff of 5 per cent and furniture a tariff of 15 per cent. Such tariff "escalation" provides much higher effective protection for the processing industry in the importing country and forces the developing country to earn more foreign exchange by increasing the tonnage of primary production rather than by adding more value to each ton. In the current round of General Agreement on Tariffs and Trade (GATT) negotiations, industrialized countries should offer to do away with tariff escalation of this kind on processed agricultural, wood, and mineral products.

The dumping of surplus products by industrialized countries on world markets can also impede sustainable development abroad. The most egregious example, disposing of hazardous wastes, banned pesticides, and other abominations by exporting them to developing countries, should stop soon as the result of negotiations now under way. Less blatant but also important is the subsidized export of agricultural surpluses, which benefits consumers but penalizes farmers in importing countries by lowering world prices. Lower agricultural commodity prices may discourage farmers on marginal soils in poor countries from making the investments in soil conservation, water management, and agroforestry that are essential to maintaining productivity. Lower output prices act like a tax on the returns to those investments, another reason for decoupling farm-income supports in industrialized countries from market-distorting interventions.

Not only can trade policies have environmental effects, but differences in environmental policies among countries can also affect trading relations. Although international "competitiveness" is of great concern to both industries and governments, it should be remembered that whenever tighter environmental standards in one country reflect higher environmental damages there, those tighter standards imply that the country has a real cost disadvantage in that particular line of production. Alternatively, whenever tighter standards reflect lower abatement costs, then they entail no loss of international competitiveness. Therefore, though the EEC has chosen to "harmonize" environmental standards to a considerable extent in creating a unified internal market, the fundamental GATT principle that domestic environmental protection measures do not distort international trade is economically sound.

Investment and technology transfer

Restoring private capital flows from Europe and North America is vital to sustainable development in Eastern Europe and developing countries. The steep decline in private lending and investment in the 1980s deprived many capital-importing countries of access to critical imports and technology and forced a severe retrenchment. The resulting economic crisis has aggravated environmental degradation in many ways: by accelerating resource depletion to increase export earnings, by driving more landless and jobless people to frontier areas as migrant farmers, and by reducing available funds for environmental protection programmes. Since private international capital movements, including capital flight, are both larger and more variable than public flows in response to international market conditions, restoring them requires joint efforts by borrowers and lenders. The United States, which has been the largest international borrower during the 1980s, must restore internal fiscal balance and thereby reduce its demands on international capital markets, lowering real borrowing costs for other capital-importing countries.

Other capital-importing countries must also create more favourable conditions for private capital flows. For heavily indebted countries, this means restoring creditworthiness, in large part by undertaking vigorous structural adjustment programmes with the assistance of the World Bank, the International Monetary Fund (IMF), and other international financial institutions. Within structural adjustment programmes, modifying policies and eliminating public subsidies and expenditures that exacerbate environmental damages, for example, can help restore fiscal balance and raise economic productivity. Member governments should see that the multilateral development banks and the IMF take full account of these opportunities in their structural and sectoral adjustment lending.

Governments in creditor countries should recognize, as financial markets already have, that current levels of debt in many countries are inconsistent with resumed growth and creditworthiness. Debt reduction negotiations in the spirit of the Brady Plan should be accelerated. Governments should explore mechanism to reduce the transaction costs of these negotiations and reduce the temptation of commercial banks to look for a "free-ride" in the process, sharing in the benefits of restoring creditworthiness but not in the costs.

Creditworthiness is a necessary but not sufficient condition for increased private capital and technology transfers. Also important are political and economic stability, reasonable predictable, and non-discrim inatory laws and enforcement policies toward private enterprise, and appropriate market incentives.

Market incentives for technology transfer include both prices and regulations. Low-polluting technologies may be available internationally, but they will certainly not be widely adopted in the technology-importing country unless its government makes effective pollution control mandatory. Nor will resource-efficient technologies be widely adopted unless resource prices in the host country reflect full incremental supply costs.

Under appropriate conditions, many investments that promote sustainable resource use and sound environmental management provide attractive opportunities for the private sector. Financial intermediation by specialized investment banking facilities, venture capital funds, and the like can help identify and realize these opportunities. Governments of industrialized countries should encourage the International Finance Corporation, the European and Nordic investment banks, the Overseas Private Investment Corporation, export credit agencies, and similar institutions to pay special attention to commercially feasible investments that promote sustainable development in Eastern Europe and developing countries.

Similarly, the World Bank and regional development banks are considering ways to channel additional resources to high-priority natural resource management projects, especially to protect biological diversity, tropical forests, regional seas, and the global atmosphere. Given the limits on members' borrowing capacities and the fact that benefits from investments in these fields are not fully captured by the borrowing country, there is a clear case for concessional terms for such loans. Member countries should support these initiatives by the multilateral development banks, and promote greater cooperation among them, since such initiatives are much more valuable to borrowing countries if donor coordination is improved.

Many of the poorest countries in sub-Saharan Africa and elsewhere, where outstanding publicly owned or guaranteed debt has been rescheduled and reduced under Paris Club agreements, will clearly need additional debt relief, as well as continued flows of new money. Paris Club members should seriously consider converting a substantial additional fraction of outstanding debt to local currency bonds, interest from which could be used to finance high priority programmes to protect human and natural resources. These resources could provide the local currency counterpart funds needed to increase capital flows for natural resource and environmental protection projects.

Managing the global commons

The most worrisome environmental problems today are large-scale disturbances to the world's atmosphere, oceans, forests, and genetic resources. Climate change, depletion of the stratosphere ozone, accelerating deforestation, and extinctions of species in the topics demand attention because of their potentially massive worldwide risks to economic welfare, health, and even life. Europe is affected by decisions taken in China, and the Soviet Union by events in Brazil, just as Africa depends on policies adopted in the United States.

Global environmental interdependence poses new challenges. Each country's actions affect itself and the rest of the world as well, but there are few institutional mechanisms through which the interest of their countries can effectively be represented in national decisions. Each country bears the full costs of its own protective measure, but captures only part of the rewards. Naturally, each country would prefer that others bear the burden of global environmental protection and share the benefits while avoiding the costs; and managing the global commons is difficult because of the "free-rider" problem. Should most countries restrict fossil fuel use to reduce carbon dioxide emissions, those that did not would gain a competitive advantage from lower energy prices while still benefiting from a more stable climate. For these reasons, responding effectively to global environmental disturbances requires international cooperation.

The 1985 Vienna Convention on the Protection of the Ozone Layer and the 1987 Montreal Protocol on Substances that Deplete the Ozone Layer provide useful models for an international framework convention and implementing protocols. They are also critically important steps to avoid climate control because chlorofluorocarbons (CFCs), besides scavenging stratospheric ozone, can be 20,000 times more efficient in absorbing infrared radiation than carbon dioxide is, molecule for molecule. Replacing CFCs with less potent substitutes might be the most cost effective step to mitigate climate change. In any event, industrialized countries should agree to phase out ozone-depleting gases by the end of the century, as recommended by the Helsinki meeting of May 1989.

Industrialized countries should also help developing-country signatories, financially and technically, phase down more rapidly. The economic rationale for such assistance is not that developing countries would suffer economic losses by phasing down CFCs. With large agricultural sectors at risk from ultraviolet radiation and climate change and relatively small industrial demands for CFCs, developing countries have much to gain on balance from rapid implementation. For this reason, non-signatory developing countries should quickly adhere to the agreements. The case for international transfers rests on the self-interest of industrial countries in helping the rest of the world phase out CFCs and adopting substitutes as rapidly as possible.

Economic instruments can help in the transition. In the short run, deposit-return or tax rebate systems could provide useful economic incentives to recover and recycle their large stock of CFCs outstanding in cooling systems and industrial processes. Moreover, taxes or fees on CFCs, whether imposed in conjunction with marketable permit systems or alone, can stimulate the development and adoption of substitutes.

The scale of the global climate problem and the uncertainty surrounding it will make international agreements more difficult. Although the emergence of the Antarctic ozone hole came as an eerie surprise, it is clear that there would be no winners from ozone depletion and that the costs of prevention are relatively modest. Similarly, the potential costs and benefits countries face from climate change are poorly understood, but the greenhouse effect is well established and documented, and scientists agree that continued accumulation in the atmosphere of trace gases that absorb long-wave radiation will eventually raise surface temperatures, with profound effects on atmospheric circulation and precipitation.

There is also no doubt that concentrations of greenhouse gases, carbon dioxide, methane, CFCs, and nitrogen oxide have increased at historically rapid rates. Extrapolations of past trends would lead to a doubling of carbon dioxide-equivalent gas concentrations in the atmosphere within the next fifty years.

To date, there are many unknowns in the determinants of climate. Among these are the roles of clouds and oceans. Clouds trap seven times as much energy as would be trapped by greenhouse gases even with a doubled concentration, but at the same time reflect eleven times as much back away from earth. Relatively small changes in the area, altitude, and water content of clouds in response to the greenhouse effect could powerfully amplify or offset to.

The oceans play an equally important role. Each year, 200 billion tons of carbon are exchanged between oceans and atmosphere, thirty times more than annual greenhouse gas emissions. Small changes in this exchange balance could overwhelm the direct greenhouse effect. Shifts in ocean currents could also trigger regional climatic change. Because of these and other important unknowns, and the complex, non-linear dynamics of the underlying geophysical systems, the effects of many other influences, and the intrinsic variability of weather patterns, detailed predictions over time and space of future climate are exceedingly difficult, if not impossible. Therefore, scientific uncertainty, differences among simulation models, and the lack of close correlations between recent weather patterns and changes in greenhouse gas concentrations are currently unavoidable.

Governments have no choice but to make decisions in the face of this uncertainty by assessing the consequences of possible future climatic states of the world and formulating policies as a response to those risks. At issue is whether those policies should be risk-neutral (acting on expected outcomes), moderately risk-averse (partially insuring against adverse risks), or extremely risk-averse (minimizing the maximum possible losses).

An international framework convention and implementing protocols should at this stage promote coordinated research and monitoring activities and a moderately risk-averse mitigation strategy. Under such a strategy, relatively low-cost measures to abate greenhouse gas emissions and slow the pace of climate disturbance would be adopted immediately, along with reasonable measures to adapt to climate changes to which past and present actions have probably committed us. A slower rate of climate change would of itself lower the economic costs of adaptation, and, by allowing more time for better understanding of the problem through research and experience, would reduce the risks of costly policy mistakes.

There is consensus that low-cost actions to abate greenhouse gases are available, though their extent is debated. The relevant measure of "cost" is one that is net of other benefits unrelated to climate change. For example, phasing out CFCs prevents health and ecological damages from ultraviolet radiation, reducing deforestation in the tropics also preserves genetic diversity, and raising energy efficiency helps with other environmental and economic problems. These "side benefits" reduce their costs as instruments for stabilizing climate.

Engineering and econometric estimates of the availability of economically feasible improvements in energy efficiency vary widely. The latter are based on past market behaviour, and implicitly incorporate all sorts of inertia, market frictions, adjustment lags, and information gaps that engineering estimates ignore. They are also based on past, rather than current or future, technological and market opportunities. Engineering estimates, on the other hand, reflect hypothetical long-run supply conditions rather than current market possibilities. The two estimates probably represent upper and lower bounds of actual possibilities.

Despite the need for an international agreement, immediate actions by a small group of countries, a "climate protection club", are economically rational. By virtue of population and economic size, the large countries, even individually and *a fortiori* collectively, would capture a substantial fraction of the benefits of their abatement actions, although benefits also accrue to smaller nations. These large countries, the United States, the Soviet Union, China, Japan, Brazil, India and (collectively) the EEC are also the largest sources of greenhouse gases. For this reason, as well as to insure themselves, these large countries should immediately adopt available low-cost policies to reduce greenhouse gas emissions by:

- Accelerating the phase-out of CFCs, among the most potent greenhouse gases;

- Promoting energy efficiency vigorously;

- Encouraging shifts to natural gas, a relatively clean-burning fuel;

- Accelerating research on non-fossil energy systems, including efficient gas turbine systems, passively safe nuclear and advanced solar technologies; and

- Promoting reforestation domestically and reducing deforestation internationally, supporting the Tropical Forestry Action Plan and other measures discussed above.

Several large countries, notably the United States but also the Soviet Union and China, have relatively low energy taxes and prices and, consequently, low average energy efficiencies by international standards. These countries should take appropriate steps to raise domestic energy prices. In the United States, the most appropriate measure would be a broad-based carbon tax high enough to stabilize greenhouse gas emissions by encouraging energy conservation and shifts in the fuel mix toward natural gas. Phased in over several years, and partially supplanting other tax sources, a carbon tax could have positive macroeconomic effects as well.

In addition to these national actions, all countries should help formulate and conclude a framework convention on stabilizing global climate, as recommended by the UNEP Governing Council, the Group of Seven (G-7) economic summit in 1989, and other bodies. This should follow closely the review of the interim findings of the Intergovernmental Panel on Climate Change in November 1990.

Proposals have been made to set global and national limits on greenhouse gas emissions and to create mechanisms for international trading of "off-sets" and emissions permits. These proposals raise serious issues of monitoring and enforcement. Tradable permit systems are not yet well enough established within countries, even for limited numbers of major emissions sources, to be readily extended to global trading among many diverse sources of greenhouse gases.

Considering that both the climate response to greenhouse gases and the extent of potential gains in energy improvement and low-cost of abatement options are uncertain, it also makes economic sense to set a maximum limit on the acceptable cost of abatement measures rather than a minimum limit on the acceptable amount of abatement to be accomplished. Greenhouse gas taxes or charges have this desirable feature: they encourage adoption of all (and only those) methods of reducing emissions that involve less incremental cost than the amount of the tax that can be avoided. Carbon taxes, user fees on CFCs, and their pricing instrument should be phased in.

Simultaneously, OECD countries should use existing mechanisms to help developing and Eastern European countries take low-cost steps to reduce greenhouse gas emissions. In particular, international financing institutions should be encouraged to channel sharply increased financial and technical resources into energy efficiency, renewable energy systems, CFC substitutes, and forestry. The World Bank and regional development banks should be encouraged to develop special lending facilities to expand investments in these fields, and member governments should be prepared to channel resources through them. Revenues from higher energy taxes and charges on CFCs represent one possible way of providing additional financial resources for these facilities.

Conclusions

The initiatives that industrialized countries can take to promote sustainable economic progress at home and abroad are varied, but share important characteristics. First, they will not require a sacrifice of economic welfare. Instead, by removing distortions in economic policies and inefficiencies in the use of natural resources, they will raise productivity and strengthen the economy, Second, they are not novel ideas. The polluter-pays principle, the goal of energy efficiency, the need to rationalize agricultural policies and reduce barriers to trade in labour-intensive manufactures have been on the policy agenda for decades. They appeared on the agenda because they made sense economically, often even before they were seen as important environmentally. Third, these initiatives still await widespread implementation. Each faces political resistance from some group that would face either short-term adjustment costs, or the long-term loss of policy entitlements. Despite overwhelming public support for policies to protect the environment, the political or institutional means have not been found to overcome or neutralized this opposition. The challenge, then, is not so much to discover what must be done to ensure sustainability. The challenge is to discover how to do it.

Chapter 6

SUSTAINABLE DEVELOPMENT THROUGH GLOBAL INTERDEPENDENCE

Ali A. Attiga*

W hat is sustainable development with special reference to the needs of the developing countries in the context of North-South, East-West relations and the need for a viable and mutually beneficial global interdependence? The concept of sustainable development has emerged in recent years in response to the adverse impact of economic development on the environment. In fact, it was only in 1987, after the publication of the report of the United Nations World Commission on Environment and Development entitled: "Our Common Future", that the concept became better known and widely used. However, the full meaning and implications of this rather complex concept leaves much room for debate.

For some environmentalists, sustainable development may simply mean ecologically balanced environmental management. Such a meaning may relegate the needs for economic growth and development to the preservation of a healthy physical environment even at the cost of economic stagnation. Others may be more concerned with economic growth and rising personal incomes with little emphasis given to sound

*Resident Representative of the United Nations Development Programme in Jordan; former Secretary-General of the Organization of Arab Petroleum Exporting Countries.

environmental management. Perhaps the core of the problem lies in the ambiguity of the concept of sustainable development. Or perhaps one might ask whether economic growth and sound environmental management are contradictory and inevitably conflictive. If they are contradictory, then how can approaches to economic development be changed to promote sound management of the environment? Or conversely, how can improved environmental management be used to sustain sound development? On the other hand, if the pursuit of development and the desire for environmental preservation are not contradictory, then where is the common bond, the mutual linkage, that holds them together? Development and environmental preservation are both separable and inseparable, contradictory and non-contradictory, depending on the time-horizon from which these questions are viewed.

Is growth true development?

In modern times, economic development has evolved as a process of human endeavour using the factors of production to increase the rate of output of various goods and services as required or demanded by the consuming public or by the authority in control of the State. Since human wants are by definition insatiable, then there is no limit as far as developmental aspirations are concerned. In fact, the continuous depletion of the planet's physical resources and the degradation of its environment have constituted the major social costs of modern development. This reflects a relatively narrow time-horizon of the current as well as of past generations. It tends to relegate environmental considerations to a low priority *vis-à-vis* immediate needs of economic development. This does not deny the huge investments for controlling air pollution in some of the large cities in the industrial countries. However, against these significant improvements, there are large numbers of cities in the developing countries where air pollution levels have long ago passed the safety margin.

What is even more tragic than the levels of pollution is the fact that despite these heavy social costs, real socio-economic progress is still very slow or non-existent in many developing countries. This means that the depletion of physical resources and the deterioration of the environment have often occurred without achieving significant levels of development. At this point, development and environmental protection (or their opposites) may become linked in a kind of vicious circle. No significant economic development on a sustainable basis can be achieved without major improvements in the environment; at the same time, such improvement cannot be accomplished without the necessary resources associated with rapid economic growth and development.

What can be done to break this vicious circle endangering the future of mankind? Should the attack be on the developmental or on the environmental front? It is obvious that in the industrialized countries, where economic development has achieved relatively high standards of living and where population growth has stabilized at low rates, the emphasis can more readily be on the environment. It is equally obvious that in many of the developing countries the most urgent need is for more rapid economic improvement. Yet, the impact of some forms of rapid economic growth and development without due regard for ecology and environmental values could very quickly jeopardize the sustainability of development and eventually even life itself. Here again, we can see development and environment as both separable and inseparable concepts. In the short run and on a strictly national basis, they have been and are still largely considered separable and distinct. However, in the long run, and in the regional and global context, they are inseparable.

Since the long run for re-establishing the ecological balance on our planet is in fact getting shorter, action can no longer be postponed. Furthermore, since the persistent economic stagnation in the developing countries has resulted in serious worldwide repercussions in the areas of international trade, debts, aid, and distribution of wealth and knowledge among nations, the future of these countries has become an international issue of global concern. Similarly, since economic and monetary fluctuations in the industrialized countries have major direct as well as indirect impacts on the fortune of the developing countries, such fluctuations, too, are of international concern. This means that people in both developing and developed countries have to change their way of thinking regarding the relation between development and the environment: whatever the differences may have been on this issue, they cannot afford any further neglect of their common interest in achieving ecologically sound development. An essential requirement for such a desirable change of outlook is the perception of development and environment as inseparable components of sustainable development. Gro Harlem Brundtland stressed this point in her foreword to *Our Common Future*, "the 'environment', is where we all live; and 'development' is what we all do in attempting to improve our lot within that abode. The two are inseparable."

The same report defines sustainable development as "development which fulfils the needs of the present without limiting the potential for meeting the needs of future generations". Here we have a concept which defines development in terms of the present and future needs of people. It combines narrow and broad time horizons, but it leaves much room for debate concerning the kind and extent of people's needs and value systems. It assumes that each generation, within a given sociopolitical system, will have the wisdom to agree on its own needs and at the same time maintain the potential for the needs of future generations. It also implies a high degree of equity in the distribution of the benefits of sustainable development within and between different generations of people. In a global context, sustainable development would require a certain level of equity of potential opportunity and a degree of interdependence between nations and different regions of the world. In view of the huge disparities in resources, standards of living and economic performance between the developed and the developing countries, how realistic is the concept of sustainable development on a global basis?

There are many who can advance a great deal of reasons against such a concept. But will those who may take this line of argument be able to convince themselves and others that sustainable development will continue to be viable in the advanced countries of the North in isolation from the developmental needs of the numerous countries of the South? However attractive and practical this alternative may seem to those who wish to maintain the status quo, it is highly doubtful that such an option is viable in the long run. The fact that such a glaringly inequitable situation has characterized the global economic scene for so long does not guarantee that it can continue to survive in the face of current and expected challenges from global demographic trends, widespread poverty, growing environmental damage, resource deple- tion, technological developments, and, above all, the persistent quest for human freedom and equality.

North-South disparity

Sustainable development is a long-term concept. It is highly complex, and is viable only in a global context of interdependence. Let us look at the state of existing disparities between the relatively few developed countries of the North and the numerous developing countries of the South. After 40 years of bilateral and multilateral cooperation for de- velopment, the average per capita income in the developing countries as a group is still only about 6 per cent of the same average in the developed countries of the North. However, as a result of significant improvements in public health, sanitation and medical care, the aver- age life expectancy in the developing countries has risen to about 80 per cent of that in the developed countries. This means that demographic pressure on scarce resources in developing countries is steadily increas- ing, not only as a result of high rates of natural increase, but also in response to the increase in life expectancy.

With more than 70 per cent of the present world population of 5.3 billion and 90 per cent of the expected population increase during this decade (estimated at one billion) in the developing countries of the South, population pressure will further aggravate the already intract- able problem of poverty in most of the developing world. Of all the well-known impediments to development on a national, regional or global scale, persistent poverty is the most serious threat to the attain- ment of sustainable development. It is the main source of poor health, illiteracy, chronic unemployment, crime, social unrest and political instability. Yet, to overcome poverty, there is no substitute for implementing effective development strategies aimed at the productive employment of human resources. But with less than 6 per cent of the average per capita income of developed countries, most developing countries simply lack the minimum resources needed for a massive attack on poverty. Thus, we have another vicious circle preventing the achievement of sustainable development. To break this circle, developing countries need massive transfers of investment funds from the affluent developed countries. Regrettably, the trend is in the opposite direction.

Primarily as a result of external borrowing and direct investment in the 1970s, the net flow of resources was positive and in favour of developing countries until 1983. But from that date onward, the net flow became negative at an increasing rate. A sample of 98 developing countries shows that between 1983 and 1988, the sum of $115 billion was transferred from their resources to the affluent countries of the North. The total net negative transfer increased from $0.7 billion in 1983 to $32.5 billion in 1988. A preliminary World Bank estimate for 1989 shows a net outflow of more than $50 billion.

In addition to the well-known legal channels of resource movements, developing countries have long suffered from illegal capital flight. An estimate of the International Monetary Fund (IMF) shows that Africa alone lost about $30 billion between 1974—1985, while Latin America lost more than $200 billion or nearly the equivalent of half its total foreign debt. At the same time, direct foreign investments in developing countries decreased from $20 billion in 1982 to $10 billion in 1986.

In the area of foreign trade, developing countries continued to lose resources because of adverse terms of trade during most of the last four decades. Although most of the world's people live in the countries of the South, their share in total world exports of goods and services are at present no more than 16 per cent. The composition of these exports is mainly raw materials, of which crude oil is the most important single commodity in terms of value and strategic importance. International prices of raw materials and other commodities exported from developing countries for the last 40 years have been mostly on a declining trend either in nominal or real terms or both. They are subject to wide fluctuation in response to market conditions.

Except for oil during the 1970s, the overall terms of trade have generally moved in favour of the importing countries of the North. According to United Nations estimates, primary commodity prices, on average, declined by about 10 per cent between 1980-1988, while international prices for manufacturers rose by some 25 per cent. Even the sharp increase in the price of oil in the 1970s, when seen against the continuous fall in its real price during the previous 20 years and again in the 1980s, did not compensate for the vast loss of depletable hydro-carbon resources, at rather low prices for about 30 years.

In the case of foreign debt, developing countries were generally encouraged by various means to increase their borrowing in order to absorb the increasing liquidity generated from the rapid ascent of oil prices in the 1970s. As most of the major oil-exporting countries were unable to absorb their sudden and vast increase in liquid funds quickly, various international banks and financial institutions took over the task of lending these funds to developing countries, particularly in Latin America. The net result of new borrowing raised the total debt of developing countries from $58.1 billion in 1970 to $1.3 trillion in 1988, with an annual interest charge of about $100 billion. As these loan obligations became due for repayment on a large scale during the 1980s, developing countries as a group became, for the first time in recent history, net exporters of capital despite their desperate need for investment funds to sustain economic development. Often lacking the resources with which to repay their debts, they are generally forced to undertake more borrowings, seek more aid and further deplete their domestic resources at the expense of their development and general standard of living. The net result is even more poverty for the majority of their people, with all of consequences of social unrest and political instability normally common in such circumstances.

New lending to developing countries, whether from commercial banks or multilateral agencies is now stagnant and declining in nominal terms. Thus in 1988, total lending was 18 per cent less than the annual lending of 10 years earlier.

The same is true for international aid, with an increasing trend towards bilateralism, various conditionalities and tied aid. In the case of foreign trade, the trend is towards greater economic integration and more trade among the developed countries of the North with a corresponding decline in trade with the developing countries. With recent changes in East—West relations, the prospects are for even greater economic cooperation among the countries of the North which may further weaken the economic position of the countries of the South.

It is evident that the situation of the developing countries as a group is already grave. Their annual gross domestic product (GDP) growth rate did not exceed 1 per cent during 1980–1988 compared with a GDP rate of growth of 6 to 7 per cent during the 1970s. Even their present meagre growth rate is unevenly distributed, with practically all the growth in GDP concentrated in China, India and South-East Asia. In Latin America, the Caribbean and Africa, economic growth has lagged far behind population increases, leading to sharp declines in per capita GDP for most of the 1980s.

Except for population pressures, all problems mentioned thus far are of an external nature, over which the developing countries have little or no direct control. In the spheres of foreign trade, aid, external debt, international finance, technology and war and peace, it is the policies and actions of the powerful industrialized countries of the North that generally determine the direction and outcome of all significant events.

The need for internal reforms

However, even if all the major external problems facing developing countries were suddenly solved, most of these countries would still have to undertake basic internal institutional and economic reforms before they could attain sustainable development. First of all, their political systems have to be made more participatory and democratic, allowing for greater individual freedom in politics as well as in economics. Their economic institutions have to be made more efficient, accountable and responsive to the social needs and the enhanced welfare of their people, regardless of whether they are public or private. Their educational systems have to be upgraded and expanded, with improved criteria for selecting the more capable students for higher education while simultaneously providing adequate opportunities for all others and thus moving towards the elimination of illiteracy.

In many developing countries, land tenure systems still need basic reforms with the aim of achieving more equitable distribution of rights and obligations consistent with the needs of more stable and productive agriculture. Most developing countries still suffer from overconcentration of land ownership, tribal land tenure, excessive land fragmentation, absentee land-ownership or all of these combined.

The skewed distribution of wealth and power in most developing countries is not confined to land. It also applies to the gains from economic development. Almost irrespective of whether these countries have followed public or private systems of ownership, the result has been more concentration of wealth and power in the hands of the few. The persistence of such a state of affairs has further reinforced the dual economy originally inherited from colonial times. The manifestation of this dual economy can be seen in certain parts of the urban sectors with modern hotels, shopping centres and generally affluent consumer groups whose interests and needs are more integrated with the economics of the industrialized countries of the North than with their own native land. Almost inevitably, these groups include the political leaders, their relatives and associates and the social élite. The other much larger and impoverished segment of the society can also be seen in the same urban centres and, of course, in rural towns and villages. As long as this kind of economic and social dichotomy continues, there will be little prospect for sustainable development to take root.

Creating the necessary conditions for sustainable development in developing countries requires a global programme to help them undertake the needed domestic reforms. Equally important, however, is the urgent need to implement a global action-oriented programme of removing all or most of the external problems facing developing countries.

Domestic reforms not only need political will and popular support, they also require the necessary resources and professional competence to formulate and effectively implement the various policies and programmes associated with such reforms. That is why sustainable development cannot take root simply by the promotion of sound environmental management. External problems and constraints associated with foreign debts, trade, aid, technology and the maintenance of world peace have to be successfully confronted. Similarly, essential domestic reforms have to be effectively implemented on a much larger scale than has so far been the case in most developing countries.

Another vicious circle

But which should come first: domestic reforms or the removal of external constraints? Here we have another vicious circle: massive external resources and assistance are needed to carry out domestic reforms; however, without these reforms no external help will bring about sustainable development. As a condition for the assistance, bilateral and multilateral aid institutions often demand that recipient countries undertake certain domestic reforms, particularly at the level of macroeconomic management. This is especially the case with the IMF and the World Bank. On the face of it, this kind of conditionality seems reasonable, but in reality it can easily miss the target. The underdeveloped state of the economy of most developing countries is such as to be non-responsive to macroeconomic management. Fiscal and monetary measures applicable in the more advanced, highly monetarized economies of the industrialized countries are practically irrelevant in dealing with the economic problems of the developing countries. An underdeveloped economy, burdened with excessive poverty, heavy foreign debts and a generally unfavourable internal and external development climate has little or no flexibility to adjust to macroeconomic demand or supply management measures. It needs basic institutional reforms and massive infrastructural and human resource investments. These are long-term investments which cannot be achieved via the conventional IMF/World Bank economic adjustment loans.

All this highlights the need to give developing countries a chance to develop by removing certain external constraints, particularly in the areas of foreign debt and trade, as a condition for their undertaking basic institutional reforms on a sustainable long-term basis. The present drain of financial resources from the developing countries must be quickly stopped and reversed in their favour. The adverse terms of trade for primary commodities should be made more equitable and then stabilized. Developing countries should be encouraged and urged to diversify their exports by giving them greater and more reliable access to the markets of industrialized countries. A growing number of developing countries with considerable export capacity and potential can benefit immediately from such a favourable policy. This could help them achieve a status of development whereby they would cease to be aid recipients and join the group of developed donor countries in a global effort to help other developing countries graduate from the list of aid recipients. This was in fact what happened with the West European countries under the famous Marshall Plan. Once they managed to accomplish the reconstruction of their economies and fully recover from the aftermath of the Second World War, they quickly became donors and partners in development aid. Prior to that, they were the recipients of massive and highly concessional aid; they also enjoyed a favourable external economic climate, particularly with the United States.

The experience of Western Europe

Although the example of the Western European countries rather simplifies the case of developing countries of today, it is worth noting some of the significant lessons from that successful venture in development cooperation. First, European countries, despite their relatively developed state of human resources and institutions, had to receive massive concessional aid and investment funds for a long time before they were able to liberalize their economies and become capital exporters and aid-giving nations. In the case of developing countries, where both human resources and national institutions are still largely underdeveloped, there is a greater need for concessional aid on a larger scale and for a longer period of time than was the case in Western Europe. Yet, as we have mentioned, developing countries have for the last seven years made a net transfer to the developed countries of the North of about $165 billion.

The second lesson to note from the West European experience is the vital importance of regional cooperation and economic integration. One of the chief merits of the Marshall Plan and its most far-sighted vision was the European Community concept. It began with the Coal and Steel Community and was gradually enlarged and carefully developed to include other sectors of the economies of its member countries, including the most difficult sectors, such as agriculture, professional services, finance and money. Initially, foreign aid to European countries under the Marshall Plan was conditioned upon their working together to forge a united front with the United States in the face of the then advancing Communist Doctrine in Europe and the world at large. No such conditionality exists today for giving aid to developing countries. On the contrary, most IMF/World Bank conditionalities require economic and political measures which aim at quick liberalization of the economy and tend to discourage regional economic grouping among developing countries. The same is generally true for much of the tied bilateral aid from the industrialized countries.

While many would agree that developing countries, as exporters of raw material, energy and primary products should organize themselves to improve their bargaining position in international markets, there are no specific regional or global procedures for assisting them to do so. On the contrary, we see a trend of resisting and discouraging such schemes. For example, when the oil-exporting countries managed to establish the Organization of Petroleum Exporting Countries (OPEC) in 1960, and when they were able to gain some control over the price of their exports in the 1970s, the industrialized countries reacted with collective vigour against OPEC and what it stood for. It was called a dangerous cartel, when in fact it was simply a loose association of mostly small and fragmented developing countries, heavily dependent on the export of crude oil. This fact was amply demonstrated when the demand for oil began to fall in response to conservation and substitution effects as well as collective demand management through the International Energy Association (IEA). If OPEC really did have the characteristics of an effective cartel, it would have responded to such a situation by sharply reducing output and keeping the price at its previous high levels. Since OPEC was treated as a residual supplier, oil-importing countries would have had to buy their residual needs at whatever the price set by the exporters. Instead, we saw how in 1986 the price collapsed from $25 to less than $6 a barrel in a relatively short time.

Thus, while most developing countries are struggling as a group of competitive exporters of few primary commodities and as importers of many consumer and capital goods, they face modern, well-organized markets in the industrialized countries. In the case of foreign debts for example, creditor countries and their financial institutions have established two well-organized groups to consolidate their positions in dealing with the debtor countries of the South. Although these two groups display strong features of cartel behaviour, they are given the attractive names of the Paris Club and the London Club!

A third lesson from the recent development experience of the West European countries is the general political ideology and framework within which they operate and even compete. Domestically, they all embrace plural parliamentary and participatory political procedures. Externally, they generally agree on the common challenges facing them in foreign affairs and defence needs. Again, the United States was a moving force behind the evolution of this favourable political climate. So far, no such situation exists in any of the regions of the developing countries. However, there are positive signs that similar conditions may eventually develop, particularly in South-East Asia, Latin America and perhaps even the Middle East, if durable peace can be achieved. In any case, the experience of Europe, East and West, proves beyond doubt that sustainable economic development can best take root in a favourable, democratic and participatory political climate.

This leads us directly to a fourth lesson from the European experience: the paramount importance of durable peace as a precondition for sustainable development. For the first time in its recorded history, Europe has enjoyed 45 years of total peace with itself and with its neighbours. With regard to developing countries, Europe's major colonial powers managed, with few exceptions, to respond positively to demands for political independence and gradually replaced their colonial role with new forms of influence and cooperation in which they still play a leading role. At the same time, regional armed conflicts, border disputes and violent internal political struggles continued to multiply within and between many developing countries to the detriment of their prospects for peaceful cooperation and sustained development.

These regional wars and local conflicts found wide encouragement and support during the era of the cold war. In the regional wars in Viet Nam, Angola, Afghanistan, the Middle East, Latin America and in other African conflicts, the developing countries were and still are the battle ground for wars by proxy. In the process, they have paid a very heavy price for their participation in terms of scarce resources and human sufferings. Moreover, they lost precious time and opportunities for establishing the conditions necessary for achieving sustained development.

The global issues

The great challenges posed by environmental degradation, international finance, trade and external debts, as well as modern technology and peace-making have by their nature become the global issues of our time. Consequently, sustained development itself has become a global concern. The developed countries of the North can no longer expect to sustain their development in isolation from the needs and progress of the developing countries. Persistent lack of development in the latter will eventually create economic and political conditions that will necessarily hinder and even reverse progress in the developed parts of the world. In other words, in the future, the developing countries may be either a powerful engine for global economic growth and development, or an equally powerful force inducing more armed conflicts and instability throughout the world. Even with the recent accord between the two superpowers and the dramatic political changes taking place in Eastern Europe and the Soviet Union, continued lack of progress in the developing countries will adversely affect economic progress and cooperation among the developed countries of the North. Their export markets will be severely reduced, and their active involvements in the regional conflicts and instabilities of the South will inevitably have strong negative repercussions on their societies as well.

The geopolitical structure

If it is agreed that all the great issues affecting sustained development are of a global nature, then the geopolitical structure within which these issues have to be peacefully resolved must be examined. Whatever the constraints within the current structures, they must evolve into a general system reflecting the global interdependence between different regions and among all nations of the world. This will require a major departure from the past, which was largely characterized by highly inequitable relationships between the developed and the developing countries. An essential feature of such a departure should be a global and systematic approach aimed at successive narrowing of the economic and technological gaps between developed and developing countries. We have mentioned several areas where urgent action is needed on the part of the two groups of countries. What remains to be examined are the resources required and the kind of regional and global institutions suitable for implementing global schemes for sustained development.

The magnitude of resources needed for more rapid development in developing countries is huge but not beyond the means of present day global productive capacity. In fact, the main problem is not simply the provision of resources, but rather the difficulty of mobilizing sufficient political will and popular support for a more rational and productive allocation of resources. For example, a mere 10 per cent reduction in global military expenditure would provide an annual sum of about $100 billion for more sustainable development. A 50 per cent reduction in the total external debts of developing countries would provide another $50 billion per annum. These two measures alone, if properly directed towards productive investment, would reverse the flow of financial resources in favour of developing countries to the tune of $100 billion per year. That would be sufficient to generate new investments and high rates of economic growth in many developing countries. Such investments will generate higher purchasing power and thereby expand the export markets of the industrialized creditor countries. At the same time, these two measures would not require higher taxes in the developed countries of the North.

Although a global consensus and an appropriate plan of action are needed for the effective implementation of these two measures, much of the power for action rests in the hands of the affluent creditor countries and their financial institutions. They must be convinced that such a global and far-sighted action is in their long-term interest. With the present and expected state of global interdependence, it should not be too difficult to realize that sustainable development requires, among other things, a higher rate of economic growth in developing countries, which in turn, clearly requires a much higher rate of productive investments.

Fortunately, for the first time in the last four decades, we have a steady and promising trend towards the reduction of global tension and regional conflicts. The radical and sudden improvement in East-West relations should reduce and eventually eliminate the alleged need for the arms race and the so-called balance of terror. Instead, we should have an intensive race for global sustainable development based on a balance of regional and global interests and responsibilities. Although it is likely that many bilateral and regional conflicts will remain unresolved for some time to come, the rapid transformation of East-West relations from confrontation to coöperation should promote a more peaceful approach to all regional disputes. In such a favourable situation, the United Nations would become more effective in performing its original function of peacemaking throughout the world.

Continued progress in the resolution of regional conflicts through peaceful means assisted by the United Nations would lead to progressive reduction in military expenditure in the developing countries. For example, a 25 per cent reduction in the total military budget of the developing countries would provide about $50 billion per year, which is more than ten times the annual additional investment needed to achieve full primary school enrolment for all the children of the world.

Conclusions

As one looks to the future, one can see a new global geopolitical structure emerging. It is a multipolar system reinforced by several regional economic powers, which will eventually compete for global status. The peaceful evolution of such a system should lead to a more balanced global structure based on a series of bridges and linkages of global interdependence: human rights and freedom; energy and environmental management; international trade and finance; modern communications; and science and technological development. These constitute the main pillars and bridges of present and future forms of global interdependence. If managed properly within a global and regional framework, they can lead to global sustainable development. On the other hand, if these strong linkages and bridges become the object of sheer competition between different economic power blocs, regardless of the overall needs and interests of equitable, global, sustainable development, then the world may simply face a new era of regional and global confrontation.

In the case of energy, particularly oil and gas, much benefit can be gained from systematic cooperation between producers and consumers. For several decades, the international oil industry was totally in the hands of the industrialized countries and their transnational companies. During that period, huge oil reserves were discovered and exploited, but the oil-exporting countries received very little return for the depletion of their most important natural resource. The result was eventually a strong reaction against this situation, which led to a series of nationalizations and take-overs by the host countries. This was followed by a sharp increase in oil prices in the 1970s, which contributed to a wave of economic instability and general mistrust between exporters and importers of oil. Then, as demand for oil declined and as producers could not agree to distribute the reduction of sales among themselves, the oil market came under the control of the buyers. This is still the situation today. However, as excess production capacity in the oil-exporting countries is progressively utilized, with no significant expansion in sight, and as the demand for oil continues to increase, particularly in the developing countries, oil prices may again undergo a rapid increase. The end result of such a situation will be a repetition of successive cycles of confrontation and economic instability, during which global sustainable development cannot endure.

Clearly, there is a pressing need for a regional and global system of cooperation based on durable interdependence between producers and consumers of oil, gas, coal and other forms of energy. If we take the case of oil and gas, which still constitute about 65 per cent of all energy consumed today, we find that the three continents of developing countries (Asia, Africa and Latin America) are all net exporters while the countries of the Organisation for Economic Cooperation and Development (OECD) are net importers. It is expected that as the Soviet Union will greatly diminish or even cease its exports of oil as it further develops and diversifies its economy. At the same time, developing countries, including the oil-exporters, are expected to increase their consumption of oil if they manage to raise their output of goods and services and improve their standard of living. If all that happens, without significant new investments in the development of conventional and new source of energy, then the world could certainly face a global energy crisis by the end of this century. Oil would just be too short a bridge to reach global sustainable development for the post-oil era.

This would be true for oil-exporters as well as oil-importers. This is a clear case where sustainable development can be achieved only through an adequate system of global interdependence. The same argument can be made for environment, trade, finance and technology. In all these cases, there are urgent needs for adequate institutional frameworks at the regional and the global levels. As we have seen, the industrialized countries have long managed to establish their viable regional institutions. In the case of Western Europe, the Single Market will by the end provide for a fully integrated common market. The OECD establishment includes in addition to all members of the European Economic Community (EEC) the United States, Japan, Canada, Australia and other countries. For cooperation in the field of energy there is the International Energy Agency. In the case of defense needs there is the North Atlantic Treaty Organization (NATO).

For most developing countries, we still have no clear-cut lines of direction regarding their regional institutions. Despite some significant achievement in certain parts of the Third World, there are still many regional conflicts and bilateral disputes awaiting settlement. Their peaceful resolution should be a top priority on the global agenda for this decade. Advanced industrialized countries should be able to realize that stable regional institutions involving developing countries would make significant contributions to world peace and global sustainable development.

At the global level, the United Nations is still our best hope for a viable institutional system of cooperation and interdependence among nations. Although membership has increased nearly fourfold since its establishment and although there are wide variations in the size and strength of its members, its vital role in dealing with global issues is generally recognized and accepted. Whatever defects the United Nations system may have, they can all be corrected through a collective spirit of cooperation and consensus aiming at sustainable development. The promotion of viable regional institutions among developing countries to balance the regional institutions of developed countries would enhance the effectiveness of the United Nations as a global centre for negotiations, cooperation and the settling of disputes. If global ideological confrontation and narrow nationalism are out of date, then there is an urgent need for worldwide recognition of the necessity for global cooperation for sustainable development based on a spirit of internationalism in place of nationalism, and multilateralism instead of bilateralism.

Chapter 7

OUR OWN AGENDA: INTERRELATIONSHIP BETWEEN THE ENVIRONMENT, DEVELOPMENT AND POVERTY*

E nvironmental problems concern us all. No nations are peripheral. The search for environmental solutions must involve the North and the South and the East and the West. On "earth" there can be no "Third World".

The interrelated challenges of development and the environment require cooperation with the North. Only together can we find solutions to: problems of international development—external debt, terms of trade and protectionism; threats to the environment—soil degradation, urban environmental problems, air and water pollution, loss of bio-diversity, climatic change, destruction of the ozone layer, and

*This paper is the introduction of the Report of the Independent Commission for Latin America and the Caribbean on Development and Environment. It has been edited by Üner Kirdar for this book. The independent commission was composed of the following persons: Oscar Arias Sáchez (Costa Rica); Miguel de la Madrid (Mexico); Oswaldo Hurtado (Ecuador); Misael Pastrana and Margarita Marino de Batero (Colombia); Arnaldo Gabaldón (Venezuela); José Goldenberg, Carlyle Guerra de Macedo and Paulo Nogueira Neto (Brazil); José Lizarraga (Peru); Shridath S. Ramphel (Guyana); Gert Rosenthal (Guatemala); and Carlos Enrique Suárez (Argentina).

management of toxic wastes; the drug problem—production, consumption and trafficking; and the potential abuse of resources of the global commons—outer space and the Antarctic. Only together can we prevent human costs of even greater magnitude.

Solidarity and complementarity

Cooperation between North and South is demanded partly because there exists an ecological complementarity between developed and developing countries. Developed countries are primarily located in the temperate regions of the world while practically all developing countries are located in the tropical ring. For the greater part, the territories of developed countries offer better conditions for agriculture than those of the developing countries, many of which are covered by deserts, mountains, and tropical forests that limit agriculture.

Developed countries produce a food surplus while developing countries must import food. Developing countries are essential partners for global environmental security, especially for the restraint of greenhouse gases and the preservation of bio-diversity. Major technological progress in developing countries would enable them to produce all the food they will require in the future without being forced to reduce the global environmental security services that they are providing. This complementarity will require solidarity between North and South. It will entail the mobilization of financial and technological resources to reach common goals. It will demand the ability to renounce a confrontational style, to forsake a mindset of winners and losers, to forget old notions of separate worlds within this single planet.

Finding peace

Humanity desires to consolidate peace. We are pleased with the relaxation of tensions between the superpowers and with the favourable environment that this brings to international co-operation. However, conventional, chemical and nuclear arms continue to be dire threats to humanity. We consider that the risk of nuclear war is still the single most important threat to the survival of humankind. While steps have been taken towards nuclear disarmament, the massive destructive capacity of the major powers remains intact. In addition to human suffering, armed conflicts still prevailing in some countries or regions cause major environmental impact on renewable natural resources and land degradation. The reduction of military expenditures is a common goal.

Past financial and ecological debts: a maze that must be straightened out

The present economic crisis and environmental threats are rooted in defective patterns of development—the economy of opulence and waste in the North and the economy of poverty, inequity and pressing needs for short-term survival in the South. The challenge is to design a strategy of development in harmony with nature and with the needs of future generations. In developing countries, the link between poverty, population and environmental stress must be given increased attention.

In our region, increasingly, we see that poverty is both the cause and effect of local environmental deterioration. This link between poverty and exploitation of natural resources helps reveal another linkage: the relationship between foreign debt and the region's environmental problems. The high interest payments on foreign debt between 1982 and 1989 led to a net transfer of capital from the region to the creditor countries of $200 billion. This has encouraged overexploitation of natural resources to meet pressing short-term needs and speedily increase exports. The 1980s have represented for the region a "lost decade". A substantial number of countries of the region have seen incomes reduced to levels reached one, two and even three decades ago. The regional gross national product (GNP) in 1988 was lower than that for 1978; the decline in the 1980s is also in sharp contrast with the previous decade's constant growth. In this context, recuperation of growth and development are necessary conditions to address pressing social and environmental issues. It is estimated that the region has an investment gap of $80 billion annually. This situation results in grossly inadequate financial investment in social infrastructure and detracts attention from urgent environmental concerns. Debt alleviation is essential for dealing with environmental problems.

The transfer of capital away from the region did not begin, of course, in the past decade. The Industrial Revolution was based in large part on the exploitation of non-renewable resources in the industrialized countries themselves, as well as in the developing countries, in a way which did not reflect their true cost in terms of conservation needs and environmental consequences. The progress of industrialized countries was thus based on deforestation and, in some cases, the predatory exploitation of natural resources. By thus exploiting nature, the industrialized countries have incurred an ecological debt with the world. This carries an obligation now to support development in order that it may not aggravate delicate conservation and environmental balances resulting from past neglect.

A common North-South agenda must include, first, the mobilization of financial resources on concessional terms to support environment and development action in the region and, second, a determination by the industrialized countries to develop and transfer environmentally sound technologies on a concessional basis. Latin America and the Caribbean are committed to the sustainable management of their ecological assets to help reverse the process of global environmental degradation and to preserve bio-diversity. However, the industrial countries must demonstrate an equal commitment to sharing the burden of the cost in a manner commensurate with their contribution to environmental degradation and their substantial ability to support and implement new environmental and development policies. The level of burden-sharing should reflect the accumulated environmental debt for which the industrial countries are primarily responsible, as well as the significant external financial support required to complement the internal efforts of countries in the region to eradicate critical poverty.

Developed countries should also facilitate access by the countries of the region to environmentally benign technologies on an affordable basis and to collaborate in joint research and development ventures aimed at accelerating the production of new and existing technologies in our countries. This will have the added benefit of helping to transform and modernize the productive sectors of the economy.

Lessons for the future

Back in history, the people of Latin America and the Caribbean were motivated by a deep, almost religious relationship between man and his environment. There have been lapses over time; but these beginnings must serve as the foundation for the region's commitment to sustainable development. The preservation of indigenous cultural identity is an important part of the region's environmental and developmental perspectives. The Indian population of the region rightly demands to participate in the strategies planned for the development of the forest which it has been using, managing and preserving for centuries.

Our message is intended for our civilian society and for its leadership. We consider that strong political will and leadership are required to break the deeply rooted popular belief that land use has no social or ecological limits; that bodies of waters are owned by individuals and are not available to benefit all society; that these resources can be exhausted or polluted with impunity; and that industry is not responsible for its wastes and emissions. Public education and participation are essential for environmental protection. Our region has experienced a democratization process that should be sustained. The broad participation of civilian society is essential if we are to achieve development with equity. There currently exists a great movement for improving the quality of our democracy in ways that facilitate people-centred development while recognizing the legitimate role of the state, particularly in its enabling and regulatory function. These processes of governmental modernization and reform should be encouraged both for their wider purposes and the contribution they can make to achieving the goals of sustainable development.

We must develop legislation and institutions to address new emerging environmental problems and threats. Old structures must be modernized and local communities and authorities empowered and granted access to environmentally sound technologies, for they are closest to the needs and demands of their inhabitants. Non-governmental organizations, especially grass-roots organizations engaged in harmonizing environmental needs and development, should be strengthened. The private sector must be encouraged to implement programmes to arrest environmental degradation before it becomes irreversible. The participation of women in environmental protection, both in urban and rural areas, is essential to promote a positive behaviour in youth and in the population in general. Major efforts should be developed in the region to achieve these goals.

We consider it essential that new economic criteria and indicators be developed that take into account natural resources as stock of "capital". We must abandon policies which encourage overexploitation of natural renewable resources; which promote the uncontrolled use of pesticides and herbicides; and which promote the inefficient use of energy. We must develop pricing and tax systems that provide incentives for environmental protection in industrial and other productive activities.

The challenge for building sane cities

Three out of four Latin Americans inhabit urban areas. An increasing number of urban inhabitants face inadequate basic services and housing and unsanitary conditions both at home and at work. The cities are plagued by severe problems of disorganized expansion, solid and liquid waste disposal and air pollution that make them vulnerable to natural disasters. This process of urbanization with insufficient capital poses an impossible task for local authorities. Thus, "informal cities" continue to grow at an accelerating rate around most Latin American metropolitan centres. For example, a city of 700,000 people is added each year to the periphery of Mexico City and one of 500,000 to the periphery of So Paulo. These cities lack the infrastructure or financial resources needed to cope with the current population or to absorb newcomers. Efforts must be made to disperse the population to medium-sized cities, but this in turn will depend on a dispersal of economic activity within a context of modern, decentralized government. The talent and creativity of the urban poor must be channelled into small community-based projects to provide housing and basic services.

Cities where industries are concentrated are often highly polluted and lack adequate social and sanitation infrastructure and proper policies for the treatment of hazardous industrial waste. Acid rain, commonly affecting industrialized countries, is increasing in industrial areas of Latin America and the Caribbean. Toxic wastes are being exported from industrialized countries and are causing major environmental problems. In several cases, industries not complying with environmental laws and regulations in the industrialized countries are being transferred to developing countries where these regulations are ignored.

The environmental challenges facing Latin America and the Caribbean concern human life and well-being. Exposure to hazardous waste presents unquestioned health risks. Seven of the 10 commonly found chemicals at waste disposal sites can cause cancer, seven can cause birth defects and five produce genetic damage. The combination of chemical residues, toxic wastes, car exhaust fumes and other consequences of uncontrolled urban pollution constitute major health threats to all, but particularly to children and the elderly.

Air pollution alone is a constant fact of life for 81 million urban residents of Latin America. The result is an estimated 2.3 million cases of chronic respiratory illness among children, 105,000 cases of chronic bronchitis among the elderly, and nearly 65 million days of work lost. The additional costs to already overburdened health care systems ultimately can be measured; pain and human misery cannot. Environmental pollution demands a concerted national and international response.

The energy dilemma

The region faces problems of insufficient energy use by large sectors of the population, emission of air pollutants, destruction of hydroelectric potential, deforestation due to over-utilization of fuel wood, overexploitation of fossil fuels and inefficient transformation and use of energy.

The production, transformation, transport and utilization of various forms of energy generate positive and negative impacts. Adequate assessment of their environmental and social impacts, and particularly the potentially adverse consequences they entail for human health, should be undertaken. The region has vast hydropower reserves and renewable energy sources. Also, the potential for energy conservation is large. The region accounts for 20 per cent of the world's hydroelectric potential; however, within the region, only one fifth of the consumed energy is produced by hydropower. While nuclear energy development in the region is limited, in some countries it may be necessary to utilize these sources in the short or medium term. In these cases, available environmentally sound and secure technologies should be mobilized. For this, the support of developed countries is crucial.

Our natural heritage: a fragile potential

The ability to meet our continent's food requirements will suffer because of increasing land degradation and the resulting decline in agricultural productivity. The rural population remains at the mercy of the fragile characteristics of the natural resource base. Rural livelihood depends on climatic cycles which affect agricultural crop production. Farm output will also be harmed in the long term by the loss of genetic resources.

Modest increases in agricultural production in recent years were due largely to the excessive use of fertilizers and pesticides derived from fossil fuels. This trend creates the fear that the gradual exhaustion of petroleum sources will in coming years cause a decline in food production, especially in the poorer countries. These countries will be greatly affected since they are highly dependent on petroleum-based products and will also face greater demands for food as their population growth rates are high. Therefore, a consistent effort to improve productivity while conserving soil and water resources is vital for the region.

The region faces water management problems. Vast arid and semi-arid areas have limited water resources. Even in areas with abundant water resources, the distribution of these resources among countries and within countries varies widely. Clean water sources in some countries have been exhausted. Major hydrographic basins exhibit symptoms of degradation. The accumulation of large quantities of sediment in these basins causes frequent flooding, resulting in serious loss of life and property. Hydroelectric plants or irrigation systems should be constructed with adequate environmental safeguards. The situation in general calls for rational and efficient water management and use. The region is endowed with vast bio-diversity. Five out of the twelve richest countries in the world in terms of plant and animal species, the so-called "ecologically mega-diverse" countries, are in Latin America: Brazil, Colombia, Mexico, Peru and Ecuador. This vital biological reserve, which is of major importance both to the region and to the world, is being rapidly depleted. The continued loss of hundreds of tropical species, many without even being classified by science, is an issue of great concern for the region. The region should ensure that this heritage, which has medicinal, industrial and food potential, generate sustainable benefits for the local population. Reforestation, rehabilitation and recovery of degraded ecosystems should enjoy top priority. Sustainable management of forests, involving other non-timber products, will promote social and economic objectives and the preservation of bio-diversity.

The Amazon: a wealth to sustain and develop

The Amazon cannot be considered simply an ecological treasure and an important regulator of global climate; it is also a major development resource. The preservation of the tropical rain forests, and especially the Amazon forest, will depend on the mobilization of research and development, technology, and financial resources for the sustainable management of this area. A commitment of support from the international community and voluntary cooperation of the eight sovereign Amazonian States is needed to preserve the Amazon as an asset for the region and for the world community.

To reach our goals, it is necessary to develop alternative technology adequate to maintain the fragile ecological equilibria of the region and simultaneously contribute to the countries' economic development. Ecological and economic zoning is a useful tool which should be expanded and promoted. The legal recognition of zoning and its close correlation with economic policies suited to the ecological reality of each zone are important elements for its success.

Preservation of the Amazon is of interest to the world community. However, it is of greatest interest to the Amazonian countries. The issue must therefore be debated by them on their own terms with the support of foreign scientists and an enlightened international public opinion. The issue at stake is the preservation of the forest and its bio-diversity, the control of atmospheric pollution and the development of the region. Agreements have already been formalized among sovereign countries of the Amazon basin. These constitute a starting point for more extensive actions.

Nature unbounded: thinking like a river

Large and small river basins, including those of the Amazon, the Orinoco and the La Plata belong to several countries. Other shared ecosystems include the Andean mountain system, the Amazon forest, the Caribbean basin and the arid and semi-arid region shared jointly by Mexico and the United States. Management of these ecosystems requires common and joint action.

Rivers, seas and oceans know no boundaries. The main problems involving the use of marine resources are overexploitation of some fish species, oil pollution and degradation of coastal resources and waterfront ecosystems, and the dumping of urban and industrial wastes and pollutants. The efficient and sustainable use of these resources would represent a major gain for the region. All coastal countries should develop coastal-zone management strategies. This is especially important for countries in the Caribbean basin and those threatened by rising seas and oil pollution, among others.

Only one sky: we all breath the same air

With the end of the cold war, humanity must address other pressing issues such as the alleviation of poverty, development, equitable relations among nations and large-scale migrations caused by poverty and the environmental crisis. Global warming will have a major effect on the rise of ocean levels and is likely to cause other climate-related disasters which will also affect Latin America and the Caribbean.

If misguided energy policies are the principal causes of global warming and climate change, we must also point out the manner in which a disproportionate use of energy by some countries, particularly the industrialized nations, causes great harm to other countries and to the balance of the planetary system. Developing countries must participate effectively in international negotiations to protect the world's climate.

Depletion of the ozone layer will increase skin cancer and eye defects and will affect marine and terrestrial organisms. The contribution of Latin America and the Caribbean to the production of chlorofluorocarbons and halons is extremely small; 95 per cent of these gases are produced by the developed world. Nevertheless, the consequences of the depletion of the ozone layer would be widely felt in the world. Industrialized countries must take measures to reverse this situation.

The production, demand, traffic and consumption of drugs is associated with health and environmental deterioration. Extensive productive lands in Latin America have been converted into cocaine plantations. Chemicals and pollutants used in cocaine cultivation and processing are dumped in rivers, spreading pollution. Co-responsibility of consumer and producer countries in this issue is essential.

The Antarctic possesses a unique ecosystem. The manner in which its rich resources should be exploited is extremely controversial. Its mineral and biological resources are desired by many nations. As a global commons, the Antarctic could provide scientific knowledge to many nations, especially in relation to climatic changes. The Antarctic

Treaty is to be renegotiated in 1991. We consider it essential that the Antarctic be preserved for use in scientific research.

The use of outer space for communications and remote sensors possesses an economic value. The geo-synchronous orbit may be considered a finite global resource which is already creating conflict because of the large number of satellites in use. The future role of this resource must be defined to ensure that its benefits be equitably shared with developing countries.

Several countries in the region have suffered increasingly from natural disasters, particularly tropical storms, notably in the Caribbean and earthquakes, notably in Central America. Disaster prevention and mitigation should become an integral part of development and environmental planning at local, national, regional and global levels. As evidence mounts of human responsibility for the intensification of such natural disasters, so does the responsibility for mitigating their consequences. There is need for such formalized sharing of the burden of natural disasters, particularly when the majority of the victims are among the world's poor.

We believe that these common endeavours must be carried out within an international and institutional framework, established at both the United Nations level and at the level of inter-American institutions. We should strive for global agreement on human actions to save our endangered habitat.

A hundred years of non sustainability: reversing a history of flawed development

The call for sustainable development has been articulated by the World Commission on Environment and Development. Its report, *Our Common Future,* asserts that humanity has the capacity to make development sustainable—to ensure that it meets the needs of the present without compromising the ability of future generations to meet their own needs. This concept, noble and sound as it may be, must be made to work in economic and social terms. To do so, we must realize, first, that some of our resources have been substituted by others and, second, that we ourselves are using some resources too fast to serve either our long-term interests or the welfare of future generations.

Although our region retains a favourable ratio between resources and population compared with other regions of the world, we recognize the immense pressure on the capacity of the ecosystems to sustain the present population growth rate.

Because our region attaches high priority to meeting the needs of the almost 200 million people living in poverty, we must regain progress and development. Development should, however, be reoriented so that growth does not aggravate pollution and environmental problems. Economic growth must not become self-destructive.

Recent action by industrialized countries to establish a modest fund to finance implementation in developing countries of the provisions of the Montreal Protocol on the Protection of the Ozone Layer is a step in the right direction. However, the implementation of large-scale and pervasive measures to redress current conditions requires that substantial additional concessional financing be channelled to the countries of the region in accordance with the specific priorities of those countries. In fact, a consensus among the countries of the region and of the industrialized world that reflects mutually agreed and beneficial obligations is essential if we are to reverse global environmental degradation and ensure sustainable development in the near future. Various mechanisms have been identified for mobilizing the required financial resources for a Global Environmental Facility. These include, among others: a "carbonsink" levy; a carbon dioxide emission levy; a tax on oil levied on the users; and voluntary contributions by the industrialized countries.

The quest for regional integration has been strengthened by growing global interdependency. Changing economic and political realities underscore the belief that strong nationalism represents a threat not only to global stability but also to the technological advances that have created a largely interdependent world, due in large measure to the speed of modern transportation and communications.

A sense of solidarity: a future for civilization

We are in the era of another major technological revolution. Its effects transcend national borders. The world is in a position to develop technologies that could render environmental degradation controllable. The industrialized nations must provide incentives for the development of environmentally sound technologies which prevent the production of harmful products and promote the efficient use of energy. A change towards a more environmentally conscious world requires that developing countries have easy and affordable access to such technologies.

The United Nations Conference on Development and Environment, to be held in Brazil in 1992, must serve as a global forum in which efforts must be made to seek a balance between meeting the needs of today and providing for those of future generations. High priority should be attributed to the discussion of those environmental issues clearly linked with development. At the heart of those issues is the urgent need to alleviate poverty and improve the quality of life of people. It is in this way that a common future for the whole world can be constructed.

Mahatma Gandhi wrote, "How can we not be violent with nature when we are violent among ourselves?" Peace between countries, peace within countries in the framework of civil and pluralistic societies, peace with nature, harmonizing satisfaction of the basic necessities of today with those of tomorrow—these are the pillars of a new kind of development, a sustainable development in terms of politics, economics, philosophy, and ethics. Our Own Agenda must be one that acknowledges the eternity of the universe. Let us move forward together and call on all those who have the willingness to act generously and who are endowed with vision and a sense of solidarity for the present and future of human civilization.

Chapter 8

GLOBAL WARMING AND GLOBAL DEVELOPMENT

G.O.P Obasi*

There are many challenges to be met as nations and peoples seek to achieve their development goals. I wish address one related area of concern, which has drawn much public attention: the impending climate change. There is now greater awareness of this issue and of the many implications it has on developmental activities.

Climate and economic development

It is astonishing how closely the economic activities of a country are tied to the climate. The crops grown and the agricultural practices, the trees that flourish, the renewable energy potential and heating and cooling needs, the water available and required, earnings from tourism, recurrence of devastating floods and droughts, many of the diseases that occur—are all affected by the climate. National activities are intimately linked with climate, but so also are trading patterns with other countries in agriculture and other commodities.

It must be recognized that present patterns of economic activity have developed over the past thousand years in a period of stable global climate. In considering the theme "Change: threat or opportunity for human progress?", one profound change that must be taken into account

*Secretary-General of the World Meteorological Organization.

is global warming due to increasing greenhouse gas concentrations in the atmosphere. Without very drastic preventive action, it is projected that this will transform the world's agriculture; change and move the forests hundreds of kilometres; create new deserts; and see the greening of some existing dry lands. The sea-level will rise and hundreds of millions of people on low-lying coasts will be seeking higher ground.

Global warming projections

To be more specific about the scientific projections, let us draw upon the recently completed assessments conducted by the Intergovernmental Panel on Climate Change (IPCC), which was formed by the World Meteorological Organization (WMO) and the United Nations Environmental Programme (UNEP) nearly two years ago. More than one thousand specialists from 60 or so countries participated in the most comprehensive assessment ever undertaken of a global problem.

The rate of change in global mean temperature predicted by the IPCC with a "business-as-usual" scenario in emissions of greenhouse gases is characterized as being greater than at any time since men first began to till the soil some 10,000 years ago. Using the best models available, the IPCC scientists predict a global mean temperature by the year 2025 of about one degree centigrade above 1990 levels, with a range of 0.8 to two degrees centigrade. By 2090, the average temperature will increase by three degrees centigrade over the globe, with a range from two to five degrees centigrade. With these projections, the earth will be warmer by about 2040 than at any time in the past 150,000 years.

The rise in sea-level, which has been one to two centimetres per decade over the past century, will accelerate to three to ten centimetres per decade, with a most likely additional increase by the end of the next century of two thirds of a metre, but possibly as much as one metre. These changes will profoundly alter the world as we know it, and the physical and biological setting for all economic and social activities. What can be done to respond to this situation?

Policy responses

The policy responses considered by the IPCC fall broadly into two categories: preventive and adaptive. Prevention involves major reductions in greenhouse gas emissions, primarily requiring great efforts in energy conservation and switching away from fossil fuels. To stabilize the atmospheric concentrations of the long-lived greenhouse gases at present levels, carbon dioxide, nitrous oxide and the chlorofluorocarbons (CFCs) would require an immediate reductions of 60 per cent in emissions caused by human activities. For shorter-lived methane, a 15–20 per cent reduction would suffice.

An international agreement for an immediate cutback of such a magnitude seems unlikely; however, a substantial gradual reduction over the next decade or two should certainly be possible. Thus, preventive strategies can significantly slow down the man-made augmentation of the greenhouse effect, giving more time for ecosystems and humans to adapt. This means that strategies to adapt to global warming and sea-level rise will be needed, as well as our best efforts at prevention.

A new ethic: a renewed opportunity

This situation is described not to create a sense of pessimism and despair, but to try to give a sense of the importance of what could be a major worldwide opportunity. The issue of increasing concentrations of greenhouse gases in the atmosphere and resulting global warming and sea-level rise evokes and strengthens new views of our world. Ever since the astronauts sent back to earth those magnificent images of earth-rise from the dead surface of the moon, the realization has been growing that our planet is a beautiful living sphere, in a corner of the cosmos where all else is lifeless. The white clouds of the atmosphere wreathe the green earth, brown soils and blue seas, all teeming with life because of the atmosphere. It is one earth and one atmosphere. Now, contamination, by human action, of that one atmosphere is causing depletion of the health-protecting ozone layer, acid rains in several large regions, widespread distribution of long-lived toxic chemicals from pole to pole and Atlantic to Pacific, and global warming.

A new ethic is capturing the minds of people in all nations—an ethic that recognizes that actions in one country which pollute the atmosphere result in effects in other countries and over the whole globe. The "democracy of the world's winds" and the delicate balance of the earth-atmosphere system are being increasingly recognized.

A global convention on climate change

WMO and UNEP are, at the request of the General Assembly, preparing the way for the negotiation of a global convention on climate change. Initial elements for such a convention have been proposed by the IPCC, and it appears that the forthcoming negotiations could be among the most far-reaching ever for both economic development and for the future health of the planet. While the negotiations will be about climate change and protection of the atmosphere, they will also be about fundamental global changes in energy policy and practices. While they concern environment, they also will address the use of the world's forests, tropical to boreal. While they deal with global warming, they must also come to grips with low-cost transfer of energy-efficient technologies to developing countries and the funding of development pathways with low greenhouse gas emissions.

This issue, therefore, should profoundly affect development strategies and must do so soon. It provides an opportunity to recapture, perhaps with somewhat different motives and in a different manner, the spirit of the great global development cooperation enterprises of the 1960s and 1970s.

Implications for development strategies

Thinking about how to combat greenhouse gas increases has led to renewed interest in improving the energy efficiency of developed countries in transportation, in industrial production, in lighting, in heating and cooling and in agriculture. It has also led to a realization that the developing world does not have to go through the wasteful and dirty consumption era that industrialized countries have followed. There are ways of leap-frogging, of using newer, cleaner technologies and of following energy-conserving pathways to development. And such development will be, in the long run, less costly and less dependent on external supplies. Among the first things that development agencies should do is to assist all countries to design energy-efficient, low-emission scenarios for economic development. Programmes to act on such scenarios should be the primary technical cooperation development challenge of the next few decades. This should not be a constraint to development, but a spur to more rapid and more sustainable development.

Consider, for example, the world's forests, which are a major "sink" for carbon dioxide. The countries of the North must manage their forests in a sustainable manner and increase the tree-covered area. So, too, should the countries of the South; but they must also develop means of meeting fuelwood needs and the requirement for agricultural lands to feed growing populations. Again, national strategies are needed to preserve some and use other forests in a sustainable manner to yield economic benefits, yet preserve the carbon dioxide sink. And such strategies must be put into action.

The recognition that adaptation to some global warming and sea-level rise will be necessary, in spite of best efforts to slow down the rate of change, also points to the need for certain priorities in development assistance. Wise adaptation measures require good prediction of the future climate, and improved prediction needs better global measurements and research. Unfortunately, many developing countries still need assistance to increase and maintain their basic climate observation networks, the measurements of greenhouse gases, and measurements which show the biological and physical responses to climate trends and changes. Many countries do not have the trained staff needed to assess scientific information on climate change and impacts on their national economies. These gaps in the global measurement networks, and in scientific capabilities, seriously impede progress in international research as well as the active and informed participation of countries in the discussions and negotiations on climate. The development of human skills to render the scientific measurements and studies truly global is urgent. In this connection, it should be noted that the traditional country-by-country approach to technical cooperation may not be the most efficient. Regional scientific cooperation is sometimes the only efficient way to deal with such matters as climate, the atmosphere, and water resources, which by their nature ignore national boundaries.

It must be noted, too, that in many countries that are heavily dependent on agriculture and natural resources, such as those of sub-Saharan Africa, economic success depends on the rains. A good rainy season means a high annual gross national product and a poor rainy season a lower one. Much can be done, through regional climate and weather prediction, to put in place agricultural and other preparatory measures to take maximum advantage of the rains as they come. In the face of issues such as this, development agencies must increasingly think regionally rather than on an individual country basis.

In summary, three clear directions for development assistance emerge:

(a) All countries must design and implement energy-efficient economic development strategies, with maximum use of locally based renewable energy sources. Technical co-operation in both design and implementation is urgently needed in many nations;

(b) Sustainable use and preservation of forests also require national planning and implementation;

(c) Scientific measurements, research and predictions of climate, the factors affecting it and the impacts of trends and changes must be supported in all countries as a basis both for wise national adaptation policies and as a contribution to global understanding. This will often require a regional approach.

Conclusions

The way in which we think of development should be profoundly altered by the realization that our planet's one atmosphere is under siege and that a major manifestation of this will be, most probably, an unprecedented climate warming and sea-level rise. For the human species, which is causing the problem, to act intelligently to deal with it requires a fundamental change in the way development proceeds in both the North and the South. Energy efficiency and increased use of renewable sources of energy must be the hallmarks of future economic development. Wise land-use, especially use of the forests, becomes an issue, not just of local or national concern, but of world-wide concern. Improved scientific measurements and understanding are essential to underpin strategies to adapt to climate change.

A blueprint for development assistance for the decades ahead can well be designed to meet these needs. Delay can be costly, even tragic. Every decade by which we postpone implementing greenhouse gas control measures commits us to a further eight per cent increase in the greenhouse effect over pre-industrial times.

The global warming issue represents a major opportunity to reinvigorate development assistance policies to address the most serious environmental issues before us and to stimulate truly sustainable economic development in all parts of the world. In this case, a positive response will benefit not only the developing regions but the whole planet, our earthly home.

Chapter 9

LIKELY IMPACT OF GLOBAL WARMING ON DEVELOPING COUNTRIES

John Topping*

O ver the last couple of years there has been mounting evidence that the human costs of rapid global warming are likely to be concentrated especially in developing countries and that some countries may be gravely affected. Climate impacts research has until recently been focused principally on a handful of more affluent countries such as Australia, Canada, New Zealand and the United States, with the exception of some worldwide agricultural studies coordinated by Dr. Martin Parry, some coastal studies carried out by the United Nations Environmental Programme (UNEP), and several country case-studies commissioned by the Commonwealth Secretariat. A government-wide study commissioned by the Chinese Government has revealed significant and largely adverse potential impacts on China, akin to those identified in the Commonwealth Secretariat case studies of Bangladesh, the Maldives and other countries.

Studies of climate impacts on developing countries are now under way on a significant scale and preliminary results are likely to be available for many areas of the world within the next year. Comprehensive studies of climate impacts in three South-East Asian countries (Malaysia, Indonesia and Thailand) coordinated by Dr. Martin Parry of the

*President of the Climate Institute, Washington, D.C.

University of Birmingham, Alabama and sponsored by the United Nations Development Programme (UNDP) and UNEP should be completed this fall. Meanwhile, a series of coastal studies commissioned by UNEP may provide detailed information on coastal vulnerability to sea-level rise in such regions as West and East Africa. The United States has also commissioned studies of likely coastal, agricultural and forestry impacts in developing countries. Preliminary results of some of the country studies carried out by the United States Environmental Protection Agency (EPA) may be available by late 1990.

The EPA-sponsored studies of likely implications of sea level rise are being coordinated by Dr. Stephen Leatherman, Director of the Laboratory for Coastal Research of the University of Maryland; the agricultural impact studies are being coordinated jointly by Dr. Cynthia Rosenzweig of the Goddard Institute for Space Studies and by Dr. Martin Parry of the University of Birmingham. The forestry studies are being coordinated by Dr. Henry Shugart of the University of Virginia.

Despite the surge of recent research interest in climate impacts in developing countries, remarkably little hard data was available, aside from that concerning the agricultural sector, to the Intergovernmental Panel on Climate Change (IPCC) in preparing its report on impacts of climate change. The IPCC was forced instead to rely on some preliminary studies, contributions by panels of contributing experts from developing countries and comments submitted in the review process in order to supplement the developing country climate impacts literature. Despite these limitations, the IPCC Working Group II in its report on the potential impacts of climate change found disproportionate impacts in developing countries. It states in its policy-makers' summary:

> "The most vulnerable human settlements are those especially exposed to natural hazards, e.g., coastal or river flooding, severe drought, landslides, severe wind storms and tropical cyclones. The most vulnerable populations are in developing countries, in the lower-income groups, residents of coastal lowlands and islands, populations in semi-arid grasslands, and the urban poor in squatter settlements, slums and shanty towns, especially in megacities. In coastal lowlands

such as in Bangladesh, China and Egypt, as well as in small island nations, inundation due to sea-level rise and storm surges could lead to significant movements of people. Major health impacts are possible, especially in large urban areas, owing to changes in availability of water and food and increased health problems due to heat-stress spreading of infections. Changes in precipitation and temperature could radically alter the patterns of vector-borne and viral diseases by shifting them to higher latitudes, thus putting large populations at risk. As similar events have in the past, these changes could initiate large migrations of people, severe disruptions of settlement patterns and social instability in some areas."

Despite the paucity of detailed studies of likely impacts of climate change on developing countries, there are a number of factors which support this IPCC Impacts Working Group II finding. First, developing countries are currently far more vulnerable than developed countries to large loss of life and destruction of dwellings from such extreme weather-related events as tropical cyclones and floods. It is quite likely that global warming will manifest itself in the increased occurrence and perhaps also increased intensity of such severe weather-related events. Although, there is no universal agreement among climatologists concerning the prospect of such an aggravation of severe weather-related events, both Hansen (1989) and Golitsyn (1989) project an increased intensity of the hydrologic cycle with greater incidence of both floods and droughts. Emanuel (1987) has projected that an effective carbon dioxide doubling at equilibrium could result in an increase of as much as 40 per cent in the intensity of the most severe tropical cyclones.

Second, by accident of geography, a large number of densely populated regions in developing countries are especially vulnerable to coastal inundation related to sea-level rise, or river delta flooding potentially aggravated by global warming. Some small island nations such as the Maldives or Kiribati could find their very existence imperiled by a rise in global sea level of only a few metres.

A third factor increasing the vulnerability of many developing counties is their dependence for energy, shelter and production on such primary resources as water, biomass and food and fibre crops whose distribution and cost may be significantly altered by climate change. Generally, industrialized countries possess a wider mix of energy sources, with much of the supply relatively immune to major disruptions associated with changed climate. Although considerable variation exists among countries, such nations tend to have considerable resilience built into their water resource systems. Biomass generally plays a less dominant role in construction in industrialized countries, and industries are often much less dependent on the availability of local sources of food or fibre.

A fourth factor underlying the vulnerability of developing countries is their relatively smaller resource base to adapt to and respond to the changes produced by global warming. As the experience of the Netherlands has shown, nations at a geographic disadvantage with respect to floods or storm surge can adapt through systematic planning and investment to protect themselves against many adverse weather-related events. Yet a nation's ability to adapt to mitigate such adverse impacts is dependent in part on its financial and technological resources and its experience in responding to similar weather-related events.

Present vulnerability of developing countries
to tropical cyclones and floods

Although industrialized countries are hardly immune to the ravages of tropical cyclones, as the damage wreaked on the Carolina coast of the United States in 1989 by Hurricane Hugo manifested, tropical cyclones resulting in large loss of human life have occurred largely in the developing world, with a very large number in the Bay of Bengal. Dr. F.U. Mahtab in his 1989 report to the Commonwealth Secretariat, "Effect of Climate Change and Sea-Level Rise, on Bangladesh," presents the summary table on the next page.

Should projections of possible increased intensity of tropical cyclones in a warmer world occur, presently vulnerable regions such as those near the Bay of Bengal, the Caribbean, the North Pacific might be especially affected. Another likely occurrence associated with global warming would be a change in tracks of tropical cyclones. This would

DEATHS ASSOCIATED WITH NOTEWORTHY CYCLONE DIASTERS

Year	Location	Deaths	Year	Location	Deaths
1970	Bangladesh	300,000	1839	India	20,000
1937	India	300,000	1789	India	20,000
1881	China	300,000	1965	Bangladesh	19,279
1923	Japan	250,000	1963	Bangladesh	11,468
1897	Bangladesh	175,000	1963	Cuba-Haiti	7,196
1876	Bangladesh	100,000	1900	Texas	6,000
1864	India	50,000	1960	Bangladesh	5,149
1833	India	50,000	1960	Japan	5,000
1822	Bangladesh	40,000	1969	India	1,000
1780	Antilles	22,000			

have a mixed effect on particular countries or regions, possibly bene-fiting some traditionally vulnerable areas while exposing other areas, including some in higher latitudes, to increased vulnerability. At this point, there is insufficient scientific knowledge to make reliable projec-tions of likely changes in storm paths. Nevertheless, an assessment of likely impacts of global warming or changing released in May 1990 by the Chinese Government (Ye et al.) projects that the high warming rate of the continent in summer will lead to formation of hot and low pressure zones, resulting in the increase of frequency and intensity of typhoon effects to the coastal area. There is, however, substantial evi-dence to suggest that increased air and sea-surface temperatures may result in some increased intensity of tropical cyclones, and should that occur, total damage associated with such storms may increase. It does not take a great leap of imagination to infer from this a possibility of overall increased vulnerability on many islands and coastal areas of the damage in tropical cyclones resulting from the storm surge. As global sea-levels rise, the base from which the storm surge begins will be higher, potentially aggravating such tropical cyclone-related damage.

A second extreme weather-related phenomenon of great concern to many countries is flooding. This is certainly not restricted to developing countries, as the severe floods in 1990 in the American states of Texas, Arkansas and Louisiana illustrate. Yet industrialized countries, such as the United States, which have become accustomed to significant flooding in some areas have generally constructed elaborate flood-control systems to minimize property damage and loss of life. Should climate change increase the risk of flooding by increasing the intensity of the hydrological cycle, perhaps also changing snow-melt and run-off, such flood central systems might be placed under severe stress. The impacts of such flooding in industrialized societies are still likely to be relatively less disruptive than in developing countries which lack such elaborate flood control systems.

Perhaps the most flood-vulnerable country of all the more populous nations is Bangladesh, which in September 1988, in the worst flood it experienced during this century found 122,000 square kilometres, or 84 per cent, of the land area submerged, with adverse affects on 45 million people, with over 1600 deaths directly attributable to the flooding and another 735 deaths caused subsequently by diarrhoea and diseases. The severe floods in Bangladesh in 1987 affected 35 per cent of the land area and 30 million people, causing over 1800 deaths. Although one cannot ascribe the recent severe floods in Bangladesh to a global warming trend, a factor aggravating the intensity of the floods may be man-made changes in the natural environment which have reduced the forest cover in the Himalayan highlands and increased the run-off to lower riparian regions.

The general circulation models (GCMs) used for predicting future climates are not sufficiently developed to provide reliable regional forecasts of changes in precipitation run-off and soil moisture. The IPCC Working Group, in its science report, nevertheless attempted using composite analyses from high resolution GCMs to make projections for five regions: Central North America, Southern Asia, Sahel, Southern Europe and Australia. Its projections for Southern Asia, 5°–30°N, 79°–5°E, point to an increase in temperature of 1°–2°C above that of pre-industrial times and an increase of from 5 to 10 per cent in soil moisture. Temperatures in the Sahel region (10°–20°NW–40°E) are projected to rise 1°–3°C above pre-industrial levels with modest soil moisture decreases in the summer in this region.

Although region-specific projections of future run-off can be made with, at best, minimal confidence, it is possible that an increased intensity of the hydrologic cycle associated with greenhouse warming as predicted by Hansen et al. (1989) and Golitsyn (1989) will mean greater occurrence worldwide of the climate extremes of flood and drought.

Geographic or physical vulnerability of developing countries

Geographic and related present physical or climatic factors make many developing countries particularly susceptible to wide-scale disruption as a result of climate change.

Perhaps the most obvious of these factors is a wide-scale vulnerability of most island nations and many significant coastal areas of developing countries to significant inundation as a result of sea-level rise. Although the IPCC has adopted relatively conservative projections for global sea-level rise an increase from the present of about 20 centimetres by 2030 and 65 centimetre by 2100 contour maps in few developing countries provide sufficient data to make projections at changes below a metre. Just as the IPCC Science Working Group was completing its work on sea-level rise, a conference of 35 top glaciologists funded by the United States National Science Foundation and meeting at College Park, Maryland, analysed ice-stream flow data from the West Antarctic ice sheet and concluded that this large ice sheet was much less stable than had been previously believed. Scientists indicated that they could not rule out the beginning of a break-up of the ice sheet within as little as 30 years. If the entire ice sheet were to collapse, this would add six metres to global sea levels over and above that attributable to thermal expansion of the upper layers of the oceans and nations of Northern Hemisphere glaciers. Accordingly, most of the studies have analysed potential impacts of a sea-level rise of one metre or more.

According to the assessment by Mahtab (1989), a sea-level rise of one metre, which he assumes would be produced by a 90 centimetre rise in global sea level and a 10 centimetre subsidence, would inundate about 22,889 square kilometres of land, about 5.8 per cent of the total area of Bangladesh. He projects the loss of 13.74 per cent of his country's net cropped area and 28.29 per cent of its forest area, with large-scale population migrations to unaffected urban areas, especially such cities as Dhaka, Chittagong, Khulna and Rajshohi. Such inundation would be likely to cause a production loss of more than 2 million tons of rice, 13,000 tons of wheat, 214,000 tons of sugar cane, 405,000 tons of vegetables, 10,000 tons of jute, 97,000 tons of pulses, 37,000 tons of oil seeds and 97,000 tons of spice, with loss of land now supporting 2.73 million cattle, 986,000 goats and sheep, and 9.73 million poultry. In this context, Mahtab's analysis is the most systematic country study done by any single individual of any country, developed or developing.

A one-metre sea-level rise would, this analysis projects, result in a loss of 1.87 million housing units, 8,273 schools, and destroy or damage 1,466 kilometres of railway track, 10,383 bridges and culverts, 706 kilometres of metalled roads, 19,772 kilometres of unmetalled roads, 148 telegraph and telephone offices, 543 electrified villages, 1,757 market centres, 375 food and fertilizer facilities, 49 health complexes and 133 health and family welfare centres.

Besides the large direct inundation in Bangladesh attributable to a one-metre sea-level rise, there would be significant additional inundation due to a back-water effect of sea-level change. Substantial inundation would be expected on both sides of the Jamuna river and of the Surma-Bouloi rivers. A one-metre sea-level rise would destroy the Sundarban mangrove forest, the habitat for the Bengal Tiger. Destruction of the forest would be likely to occur well before the inundation due to an increased salinity level.

Although not as detailed as Mahtab's analysis, the recent Chinese Government assessment projects extensive coastal damage in China from a similar rise in sea level. Sea-level rise is likely to cause loss of most of the existing salterns and sea-water fish breeding farms, a major food base for China's coastal cities. Nearly half of the area of the Pearl

River Delta, about 3,500 square kilometres, will be inundated, with large destruction of the more developed areas on the Yangtse River and the Yellow River and a loss of at least 10 million tons of grain. Sea-level rise can also be expected to produce adverse impacts on housing, transportation and the water supply, with salty tides intruding into inland areas.

An analysis of the effects of carbon dioxide doubling done in 1989 by the Indonesian Ministry for Population and Environment showed that a one-metre rise in Bekasi Regency would flood about 7,000 hectares of brackish water fish area, damage 10,000 hectares of food crops through salt water intrusion, and displace 3,300 households from their land. Such a sea-level rise in Karawang Regency would flood about 11,000 hectares of brackish water fish areas and damage 50,00 hectares of food crops and cost 80,000 households their livelihood. A one-metre sea-level rise in Subang Regency would, the study projects, inundate 7,000 hectares of brackish water fish areas, damage 29,000 hectares of wetland rice and 6,000 hectares of home gardens and destroy the livelihoods of 81,000 farmers.

Some small island nations might face extinction with a rise of only a few metres in sea level. This is potentially true of such countries as the Maldives and Kiribati.

A second element in the particular geographic vulnerability of many developing countries is their location in the monsoon region. A change in the monsoon patterns could greatly affect the way of life of such nations as India, Pakistan, Bangladesh and many African countries as well. Changes in the monsoon could result in flood or drought or both. Little is known at this time about how global warming may affect the timing of the monsoons or the occurrence of the El Niño Southern Oscillation (ENSO) phenomenon, both of which greatly affect the climate in the low latitude regions in which so many developing countries are situated. It is quite plausible that a rise of only one degree centigrade in the temperature might affect both the pattern of the monsoons and the ENSO and that the impact of such changes might dwarf the direct impacts of such a temperature rise.

Potential impacts on developing countries of climate-induced changes in the availability of energy, biomass, food or fibre

In its policy-makers summary, the IPCC Working Group II on Impacts has found that global warming can be expected to affect the availability of water resources and biomass, both major sources of energy in many developing countries. These effects are likely to differ between and within regions with some areas losing and other areas gaining water and biomass. Such changes in areas which lose water may jeopardize energy supply and materials essential for human habitation and energy. Moreover, climate change itself is also likely to have different effects between regions on the availability of other forms of renewable energy such as wind and solar power.

The recent Chinese Government impacts assessment has projected potentially severe adverse effects on Chinese water resources and biomass as a result of global warming. Despite China's large share of the world's population, it has only about 5 per cent of the volume of the world's fresh water resources, one of the lowest per capita volumes of any country. The Chinese assessment projects that global warming will result in significant decreases in soil moisture in winter in south China and substantial decreases in soil moisture during summer for all areas of China except east China and south China. Currently, water resources tend to be scarcest in winter in south China and the northern coastal areas and to be scarcest in the summer in northern China and the middle and southern parts of the country. The projected changes are likely to aggravate an already severe water supply problem.

The anticipated reductions of soil moisture are also expected to produce large reductions in major tree species. The Chinese analysis indicated that global warming and related changes in soil moisture would be likely to decimate or severely affect four of six principal timber species in China. *Pinus Koraiensis,* which has weak resistance to natural calamities, can be expected to suffer from increased forest fire incidence during the spring and autumn dry period in north-east China. Extremely adverse impacts are predicted for *Cunninghamia Lanceolota,* which supplies about a fifth of China's current output of commercial timber. This species grows through subtropical areas of China and flourishes best in a temperature range of 20° to 26° C. High summer time temperatures could be expected to cause the death of this species over a large area. *Pinus Masoliona,* which accounts for half of the forest reserve in the provinces of south China is expected to retreat southward on a large scale with a decline in production. Very extensive losses are projected for *Pinus Yunnaniensis,* the major species of timber trees in the south-west of China. Increased temperatures and reduction in rainfall are expected to cause much of the growing area of *Pinus Yunnaniensis* to turn to steppe.

Owing to the wide variations in projecting regional changes in precipitation and soil moisture, there are great uncertainties inherent in country-specific projections of agricultural production in a warmer world. Some regions would be likely to gain and others to lose as a result of a combination of impacts on agriculture, including higher temperatures, elevated carbon dioxide levels, changed growing seasons, altered precipitation, run-off and soil moisture, changed storm patterns and inundation of some coastal and river delta agricultural areas by sea-level rise. To the extent there would be gains, they would be expected to occur largely in the higher latitudes, generally in developed countries which might experience longer growing seasons. Adverse impacts would be especially concentrated in the lower latitudes, where so many developing countries are located. One of the most severe of these potential impacts is heat stress on major food crops such as rice, wheat and corn. Should maximum summer day-time temperatures rise significantly, in some areas rice production of even the more heat resistant species could become problematic during the hot season. Changes in temperature in combination with alterations in soil moisture and run-off could significantly affect agricultural yields in many developing countries. The recently completed Chinese climate study predicted differential impacts on agriculture among regions, with some gaining and others losing, but an overall aggregate loss of at least 5 per cent in national agricultural production.

Besides the direct effect of changes in food production on availability and price of food for consumption, climate-related changes in production could also trigger large movements of people from rural areas to already crowded cities. Furthermore, changes in the relative price and availability of energy, water, biomass, and food and fibre crops will affect the competitive position of many developing country industries dependent on significant use of such resources.

Resource limitations of developing countries in responding to climate change

Besides their potentially greater vulnerability to adverse impacts of climate change due to geographical, climatic and economic factors, developing countries generally have more limited resources to respond or adapt than most industrialized nations. Options such as dike construction and maintenance which may be available to an affluent country such as the Netherlands may prove too costly for some vulnerable low-income countries. Many developing countries such as Egypt, Bangladesh, India and China have had experience over hundreds of years in responding to the ravages of flood and drought. Generally, there is no lack of technological know how in such countries for buffering against such climatic disruptions. Other developing countries such as small island nations facing the prospect of significant coastal inundation due to sea-level rise may have relatively little experience in designing and implementing such responses.

The development of effective strategies for preparing developing countries to cope with climate change may require some outside assistance consisting of various combinations of investment capital, grants or loans and provision of technical cooperation.

Adjusting development cooperation strategies to factor in climate change

By almost any reasonable analysis, rapid climate change would create disproportionate burdens for developing countries, in some cases possibly severely affecting the social stability of entire nations. The build-up in concentrations of greenhouse gases underlying this projected (and perhaps already occurring) climate change has come to date largely from the more affluent nations of Europe and North America. Global mean annual surface temperatures have risen about 0.6° C in the last century. Disagreement exists within the scientific community as to whether this warming trend is a signal of a long-term greenhouse warming or merely a fluctuation within the range of normal climatic variability. The United States, for example, produces 21 per cent of the current global load of greenhouse gas emissions and has produced an even larger proportion of past global greenhouse emissions. The two other largest sources of greenhouse emissions are the Soviet Union and the countries of the European Community.

An equitable argument can certainly be constructed that nations of the industrialized world, having set in motion changes in the composition of the earth's atmosphere which will profoundly affect the future of humanity in many countries, have a moral and perhaps a legal obligation to assist in mitigating these adverse effects. Already this argument is being pressed vigorously in greenhouse and stratospheric ozone depletion discussions by countries such as Brazil and India.

Besides the equitable and humanitarian arguments for some concerted effort by more affluent nations to assist vulnerable developing nations to respond to climate change, there is a compelling practical argument. Future population growth is expected to occur largely among those nations now characterized as developing countries. These countries generally have far smaller per capita energy use patterns than is characteristic of most industrialized nations. Should their populations grow as projected and be accompanied by a change in energy use comparable to that of the industrializing phase of currently affluent countries, greenhouse gas concentrations would rise to levels which would pose enormous risks to all humankind, possibly telescoping into the next century a warming as great as that which has occurred in the 18,000 years since the peak of the last ice age.

Such rapid change would be an almost certain ecological disaster for industrialized and developing countries alike, with movement of climatic zones greatly outstripping the ability of vegetation to migrate, thus destroying the habitat that sustains much of the plant and animal life of our planet. Although the impacts on human settlements of such rapid change would likely be most severe in developing countries, coastal cities of the industrialized world, such as New York, Charleston, Miami and New Orleans, Leningrad, London and Tokyo, could be severely affected. If current indications of the possible instability of the West Antarctic Ice Sheet are borne out, the case for concerted cooperative action by all coastal and island nations becomes overwhelming.

Already some modest steps have been made towards such cooperation. At the recent London meeting which developed an international agreement to accelerate the phase out of chlorofluorocarbons (CFCs) and other substances damaging the stratospheric ozone layer, an initial sticking point had been the creation of a fund to finance the transfer of substitute technologies to developing countries to allow them to reduce or eliminate harmful emissions while still pursuing economic growth. The United States initially resisted such an initiative; however, it reversed its position and agreed to finance 25 per cent of a fund jointly administered by representatives of developing and industrialized countries. A sweeping stratospheric protection agreement was achieved with prospects that India and China will both sign this agreement.

Although negotiations on greenhouse gases have not yet begun in a formal sense, at least one major industrialized country has begun to pursue an aggressive programme of assisting developing countries in coping with climate change. Japan will provide $2.25 billion over the next three years to developing countries in environmental assistance. With the participation of other nations in the Asian Pacific Region the Japan Environment Agency (JEA) has begun to develop a regional action plan to respond to climate change. The JEA has already attracted the active support of Japan's development assistance agencies for this effort and is seeking similar participation from the Asian Development Bank, the World Bank and United Nations environmental and development agencies.

Although the elements of such regional cooperation are still being worked out among the participating Asian Pacific countries, they may include some combination of cooperation, including funding, of better monitoring of changes in sea level, vegetative cover, sharing of satellite data on storms and funding and pooling of research on such critical issues as relationships among global warming, monsoon patterns, occurrence of the ENSO phenomenon and changes in the frequency, intensity and storm paths of tropical cyclones. Regional cooperation could also extend to such areas as sharing of coastal engineering know-how to respond to sea-level rise and development of more energy-efficient strategies, an area where Japan stands out among the industrialized nations.

Japan envisions a series of cooperative actions extending from Pakistan on the West to the small Pacific Islands on the East on very practical steps to enhance response capability. Policy-makers from the region could assemble annually to update and refine their cooperative regional action plan.

If this Japanese initiative is successful, it is likely to have several broader implications. First, the plan should already directly benefit more than half of the earth's population and nearly 60 per cent of the population of the developing countries. Second, by breaking the global climate issue into more concrete practical approaches among similarly affected neighbouring nations, it may foster more rapid cooperation than is possible in a more global arena. Third, an Asian Pacific region cooperative action plan could be instrumental in ensuring the success of the United Nations Conference for Environment and Development (UNCED) set for June 1992 in Brazil. Many observers view this meeting as a likely site for the signing of a climate framework convention and a forestry conservation protocol. Achievement seventeen months before of a region-wide understanding embracing five of the eight most populous developing nations should greatly facilitate the prospects for the success of UNCED.

As the first systematic effort to mesh climate response strategies with development cooperation programmes, the Nagoya meeting provided preliminary answers to some sensitive questions that face development planners who have recently begun to confront the challenge of a likely rapid and large-scale climate change. Should major development projects be discouraged in coastal areas which appear vulnerable to inundation from a modest rise in global sea levels? Should concern over future agricultural emissions be factored into the planning of large-scale agricultural projects? Should development financing agencies seek to encourage renewable energy sects or use of more hydrogen-rich fuels such as natural gas in order to limit growth of greenhouse gas emissions? Should development assistance programmes seek to limit greenhouse emissions in the transportation sector by encouraging some combination of mass transit, vehicle emissions controls, use of fuels such as ethanol derived from vegetable wastes, or greater urban facilities for bicycling?

One thing became clear to this author during a recent visit to Indonesia, Thailand and Bangladesh: there is a remarkable amount of know-how in developing countries on the best means for both the adaptation and limitation of future emissions. It would be a serious mistake in our focus on the problems of financing the transfer of technologies to fail to recognize and build on the solid base of local know-how. Perhaps the most effective of all greenhouse and forest conservation measures in Bangladesh would be an improvement in the burning efficiency of the *chula* or cooking sleeve, a minimal cost innovation developed by Bangladeshi scientists. A major role of development co-operation institutions should not merely be arranging the transfer of technology, but building up the indigenous capability of environmental and energy institutions in developing countries. A strengthening of such institutions may also simultaneously serve the dual objectives of safeguarding the environment and ensuring the development of improved economic conditions for a nation's citizens.

Chapter 10

LONGER BROOM HANDLES

Harriet B. Crowe*

One kind of change

Scientists, policy-makers, politicians, government leaders and informed citizens in countries around the world are increasingly convinced that human activities are changing the global environment in ways that will profoundly affect our daily lives. With this increased conviction has come a growing recognition that not only does global change itself have to be understood and better predicted, but that strategies to adapt to and mitigate it should be pursued.

The relative rapidity of the change under way is one of its most dramatic aspects. Through the examination of paleo records (pollen deposits in peat bogs and trapped bubbles of gases such as carbon dioxide and methane in ice cores, for example), it has been estimated that the present rate of heating ranges somewhere between 0.2 to 0.5 degrees Centigrade per decade. This is from four to ten times as fast as any earlier changes.

In addition to the overall rapidity of global change, the regional effects likely to ensue are important for humankind. For example, some speculate that the frequency of severe weather events—tornadoes, hurricanes, typhoons—will increase, as will their severity, and that fluctu-

*Vice-President of the University Corporation for Atmospheric Research, Colorado.

ations in weather patterns producing droughts or floods will become more extreme. It is also speculated that growing patterns will change, in some cases dramatically. If the climate conducive to the growth of certain trees, for example, shifts to the north faster than the trees can migrate northward, whole forest species may disappear. If precipitation and evaporation patterns change, arable land may become barren, and vice versa. The type of crops suitable for cultivation in particular regions will also be affected as precipitation patterns shift. Other impacts affecting habitability are likely, such as the quantity and quality of an area's water supply. Worries about the loss of biological species abound, as do concerns about the impact of a rise in sea-levels. It is estimated that the sea-level rise will be ten times as fast as that ever experienced, reaching levels by the end of the next century about a metre higher than today. Some studies indicate that in the United States half of the present wetlands will be lost. Growth in coastal populations around the world is cause for significant alarm.

Although humankind is notoriously adaptive, it seems certain that the magnitude and globality of the possible impacts are unprecedented. And the environmental change we face may well prove to be the paradigm for other changes of equal importance. Can we turn these changes from potential threats into opportunities? I believe so.

Some connections

The effluent of man-produced greenhouse gases, associated with northern-hemisphere industrialization and worldwide population growth, is at least a major contributor to the anticipated climate change. Indeed, a strong body of opinion exists that these are the primary drivers of such change. A graph famous in some circles and familiar in many more, documents the growth in atmospheric carbon dioxide in just the past 30 years. These measurements, taken at Hawaii's Mauna Loa Observatory, in air pristine by any standards, shows the steady rise in atmospheric carbon dioxide in just 30 years. Carbon dioxide is one of several gases that trap radiation and can lead to heating of the earth's surface; it is directly traceable to the increased use, during that same period, of fossil fuels.

Humankind's use of the planet's resources, in search of comfort, food, clothing and profit is now affecting the planet's system in sufficient degree that the planet's own cleansing techniques can no longer fully cope. Unrestrained exploitation of forests, thoughtless use of fertilizers and fossil fuels and zealous insistence on the right to procreate are leading us to a world in which living conditions will be drastically different. Richer countries will feel the effects of the differences on a much slower time scale than poorer countries, where rapid population growth, illiteracy, poverty and starvation are the norm, and where the possible threat of climate change some years down the road is completely meaningless.

What, then, is there to be done?

Some helpful steps

In the *Ugly American,* Lederer and Burdick place American citizen Emma Atkins in the village of Chang 'Dong in the imaginary South-East Asian country of Sarkhan, where she noticed that all of the old men and women suffered from badly bent backs, to the point of being crippled. She also observed that they swept their homes, yards and pathways each day after the monsoon with brooms that had short handles, accordingly requiring them to bend over at the waist to wield the broom. After sustained use of these brooms, the old peoples' spines became permanently adapted to the posture demanded to keep their living places clean. Emma's approach was "low-tech", low cost and relatively slow to carry out; but she succeeded in improving the lot of the older people in the village by herself using a longer broom handle and showing that the bent backs they had always suffered from were not preordained. While this story is itself fictional, it is based on a factual situation.

In this context, the recent work of Walter V. Reid, James N. Barnes and Brent Blackwater is of particular interest. Their findings were published in 1988 by the Environmental Policy Institute and the National Wildlife Federation under the title *Bankrolling Successes: A Portfolio of Sustainable Development Projects.* The volume summarizes twenty such "short-broom handle" projects from establishing windbreaks in the Majjai Valley in central Niger, to the restoration of the Sukhomajri watershed in northern India, to the improvement in the charcoal stoves used by families in Kenya. On page 2 of their introduction to this report, the authors say:

"Planners have long ignored the importance of including locally affected people and knowledgeable non-government organizations in the planning process. Their participation has both moral and practical implications".

I believe that if progress is to be made in responding to change, it will necessarily depend on a very mixed strategy, from providing the sweeping men and women of the world with longer broom handles to humane adaptation of the massive, powerful technologies now available. The solution will have to be as complex as the problem; and in certain instances as simple. The moral I take from Emma's story is that "low-tech", culture-sensitive steps should be pursued in parallel with the more exotic approaches that will also be required.

Energy-efficient techniques should be exploited in countries able to carry them out and should be exported by these same countries to the developing world. Nations of the northern hemisphere, having achieved a relatively high quality of life for their citizens, should be required to participate in such exploitation and exportation; tax credits, trade policies, moral suasion and international agreements should be brought to bear.

Foreign assistance should be deployed as a tool to aid humans in meeting their fundamental needs, such as nutrition, shelter, health, independence (self-determination) and education. At the same time, it should be recognized, and decisions taken accordingly, that in meeting fundamental needs one is also aiming to bring about changes on a local scale essential to realizing national, international and global-scale needs.

This may be most especially true with respect to adopting strategies to mitigate climate change and its potential regional affects.

Technologies and development promoted in developing countries should be of a scale that is proper and appropriate to the recipient country, and recipients should have a say in what that is. Development strategies must take genuine account of indigenous cultural needs and values. Measures of success of aid programmes should be germane to the recipient culture. And here, of course, we encounter a paradox of major proportions: some of the changes viewed as essential (such as population stabilization) run directly and strongly counter to important, deeply-held established values in different cultures. A change in the values themselves is required. The appropriateness of achieving the change can be measured in terms of the greater good. But how does one correctly and sensitively negotiate such a change?

It cannot be forced on a society or culture; it must occur with the participation and conviction of the people who will carry it out. The *Bankrolling Successes* publication mentioned previously describes a family planning programme in Zimbabwe, which overcame very strong social, political, legal and economic constraints that militated against any family planning, specifically the use of contraceptives. The success (measured by a significant increase in the use of contraceptives between 1981 and 1983) is attributed to the growing strength of the women's movement in Zimbabwe and to the local involvement through a network of 637 community-based distributors, almost all of whom are married women with children (and using contraceptives themselves).

Sustaining the health of children and mothers is of the highest importance and is an essential first step leading to limiting population growth as a matter of individual choice. Healthy mothers whose babies are healthy tend to have fewer children. Government support for population growth management, perhaps expressed as funding for nutrition, and prenatal and postnatal care should be a matter of policy.

Management of resources, restoration of resources, and fair and just distribution of resources must be striven for. International protocols, special action assistance and interest programmes, transnational development groups—all current and perhaps some as yet unforeseen methods of cooperation to provide the federal level of support for individual, community, regional and national efforts should be pursued. For most people of the world, the environment—the land, water and soil—is the only economic resource they have. Its protection should be of the first priority.

Education about human rights and responsibilities, equality of opportunity, and dignity for all individuals, and especially for women in cultural and professional systems are essential.

Other kinds of education of equally high priority include rudimentary levels of knowledge and skills. How can we expect people who do not have enough food to eat, nor a place to live, nor acceptable freedom from disease, to worry about the future of the globe 100 years from now? How can we expect people in cool climates and in much better circumstances to worry about that when a couple of degrees warming sounds positively benign? Should we start talking about the "inferno influence" rather than "global warming"?

All individual efforts should be rewarded and encouraged—recycling, biking and boycotting products of recalcitrant corporations.

Some myths and near myths

There are statements made with regularity, including those in some of the materials distributed for this Round Table, that I believe need closer examination.

We can't do anything about it. Clearly we can do something about "it." We are doing something about "it" in many quarters around the world. We know what to do about "it" in many, many instances. The complexity of making the changes we need, to adapt to the changes we face is staggering and can cause both systemic and individual incapacity to act. However, many enlightened municipalities, governments, private foundations, lending institutions, research scientists, industries, individuals and policy groups are taking steps to learn, educate and prepare for the future in a thoughtful manner.

One example will suffice: the Foundation for the Development of Polish Agriculture, established by the Ford Foundation and other philanthropies in the United States and Western Europe, combines, it seems to me, the right touches at several levels: private funds, research efforts, local education efforts, direct involvement of the Polish farmers, low-tech (tipping trailers for hauling and delivering farm produce, and liquid manure tanks), management of the programme by the Poles, and return of profits to the participants.

Adapting is too expensive and disruptive. Yes, adapting will be very expensive and disruptive but not as expensive as not doing so. The expensive and far-reaching changes must be paced properly and negotiated among those they will impact. But somehow we must move now towards a new global moral imperative emphasizing long-term, humane policies and plans.

Economic improvement of living conditions in developing countries must track that of the northern hemisphere. Build big and the benefits will trickle down. This is my paraphrase of the view promulgated by many statements in respect to economic development around the world. Why must we assume continued economic expansion, especially at the same rate as in the developed countries until now? Can we not imagine a stabilized world economy where benefits are more uniformly distributed? I am not suggesting that distribution of wealth and earnings should be on any across-the-board formula for each individual. There will always be skills and talents in our world that are more valued or needed than others, and the reward structure should reflect that. But I do believe that the extreme gaps existing between rich and poor today need specific attention and correction.

The trend to increased urbanization of the globe, and the attendant move of populations to urban areas, is irresistible. Why? I read that "Since most of the growth in populations will occur in the urban areas of the developing world, urban air quality will become increasingly crucial to human health."[1] I also read that this trend ". . . will intensify the need for and the difficulty of supplying basic services and maintaining infrastructure in large urban areas."[2] And, "All too often, expansion into new and marginal agricultural land is, out of basic necessity, led by those least able to overcome its difficulties or to farm it in a sustainable manner."[3] It seems to me that these are really counsels of despair and this suggests that their premises are subject to examination. Perhaps conditions now existing and making us believe these "myths and near myths" can be changed. Can we not envision assistance aimed at making rural areas attractive to the best and strongest of our young people, perhaps slowing over the long term the trend for these people to move to the urban areas in search of quicker gratification? Several projects described in *Bankrolling Successes: A Portfolio of Sustainable Development Projects* indicate to me this is not a pipe dream.

Conclusion

These considerations argue for a concerted approach by all the nations of the world to the problem of achieving and sustaining a decent life for the planet's inhabitants. We know that indiscriminate pollution of the environment, unrestrained population growth, and careless misuse of our natural resources will lead to the neglect of fundamental human needs. And only if those needs are met are we likely to achieve the level of local and global commitment that will be required to manage our environment in a productive way.

Complex strategies are clearly called for; simple solutions should not be ignored, however. I believe the challenge is before all of us to turn the threats we surely face into opportunities.

> There is a cyclone fence between
> ourselves and the slaughter and behind it
> we hover in a calm protected world like
> netted fish, exactly like netted fish.
> It is either the beginning or the end
> of the world, and the choice is ourselves
> or nothing.
>
> Carolyn Forch
> *Ourselves or nothing*

Notes

1. *Our Common Future: Report of the World Commission on Environment and Development,* Oxford and New York, Oxford University Press, 1987, p. 5.
2. *Ibid,* p.2.
3. *Ibid,* p.6.

Chapter 11

TECHNOLOGY AND ECOLOGY

Heitor Gurgulino de Souza*

Many global concerns have emerged over the last decade on the international agenda with increasing intensity. I highlight three for present consideration: (a) the threat of the ecological balance of the earth; (b) the challenges deriving from new technologies; and (c) the capacity of developing countries to respond to these changes in a way that allows them to attain a sustainable basis for development.

Almost three decades ago, a social scientist, Karl W. Deutsch addressed the importance for political systems to include new information—and this involves all factors related to "change"—into the decision-making process. He developed a concept of learning which has—in light of the recent political upheavals in some parts of the world—gained new validity. Deutsch introduced two terms, "creative learning" and "pathological learning".[1] The former meant the ability of political systems to digest new information as an integral element of the decision-making process, to renew the system where necessary and to make pragmatic choices accordingly. The latter, on the other hand, referred to the inability of political systems to allow new and emerging developments to influence policies which—in the long term—implied learning through negative experience and the ultimate failure of the system.

*Rector of the United Nations University.

New technologies play an important role in the growth of nations. At the same time, concern for our environment has risen to a previously unexpected level. Information on new technologies and on the changing environment have therefore become a crucial factor in the decision-making process and cannot be ignored by policy-makers with a sense of responsibility for a sustainable future.

Technology: impact on human development

In conceptualizing the future tasks of UNU's new Research and Training Centre, the "Institute on New Technologies", a thorough survey was undertaken to identify the most crucial research gaps with regard to the current technological development in areas such as micro-electronics and biotechnology. It is well known that the knowledge of the application of micro-electronic-based innovations in many developing countries is still rudimentary. Research on the actual development and transfer of such technologies from the industrialized countries is still very limited. And the possibility of linking them to local technological skills needs further study. Research on the output, employment, regional distribution and trade effects of micro-electronic technologies in the developing world leaves a lot to be desired. Most studies on these questions have focused on the sectoral impacts, overlooking the intersectoral implications. The gap between research and policy-making is still significant.

Future research in this field should focus on the following:

(a) the relationship between the implications of existing trends in the technological revolution and the formulation of development strategies;

(b) the importance of identifying alternatives of technological development better suited to the actual needs and conditions of the developing countries.

A systematic exploration of the desirable directions of new technological developments more appropriate to the policy context and resource environment of developing economies is necessary. The gaps between current research on new technologies and the needs of policy-makers in deciding on the general framework for science and technology policies, including the selection of priorities, must be filled. Closer links between technical research and the economic and social science disciplines must also be fostered in order to produce data and information useful for the decision-making process. Here we can already draw on some of the research undertaken in the industrialized countries and make use of the results of such research to benefit developing countries. Research on the impact of technological change on the environment in developing countries, for example, could be very useful in preventing the negative effects of the industrialization process which have affected the developed world.

A closer look is needed at the actual and specific needs of developing countries. Biotechnology may well hold the promise for new medications to fight some tropical diseases common in the developing countries. Yet, owing to a perceived lack of commercial interest, the relevant research is not being undertaken in the industrialized countries. Building up research capacities to meet these specific needs will indeed be a challenge for the developing world. Likewise, application of technology could have a dramatic impact not only in combating drought and desertification, environmental degradation—such as deforestation and soil erosion—but also in better coping with natural disasters. Soedjatmoko once said:

> "Development succeeds when a society as a whole and at all levels learns to make use of its resources through the application of science and technology to improve the daily lives of its citizens in ways that are consonant with their basic values and aspirations."

The fact that technology strategies and policies are not just a matter of foresight and good management of resources must be recognized. Such strategies can succeed only if the actual needs of the people affected by the changes they bring about are taken into account. Information on these needs is an important element which has to be considered in the creative learning process of policy-makers.

Ecology

Concern for the environment is reflected in different approaches towards global environmental change. The first one is an attempt to reconcile development and conservation in a specific region. Jacques Ives and Bruno Messerli, two of the world's leading experts on mountain environments, undertook a thorough study on mountain ecology as part of UNU's work in this area.[2] The prediction by the conservationists and scientists over the rapid deterioration and the irreversible environmental supercrisis of the Himalayan region was investigated and some interesting conclusions were reached. Our study revealed a rather complex pattern: while some of the concerns commonly expressed proved valid, the overall theory of environmental degradation which our researchers had adhered to in the beginning of the project did not hold. Likewise, some of the correlations that had been represented as cause and effect could not be upheld. Thus, the major elements commonly regarded as causes for the environmental degradation—population growth and deforestation—seemed to be of less importance than originally assumed, in particular with regard to some of the problems in the lowlands that were attributed to them. The researchers argued, therefore, that if reforestation in the mountains is conceived as the sole palliative to the problems of the plains, vast resources will be expended to reap only disappointment.

Moreover, this notion may divert attention from the necessity of water resources management and adaptation to the natural environment of the plains. By focusing on the linkages between mountains and plains as a whole, rather than on the mountain region alone, the researchers were able to challenge common assumptions and bring new ideas and concepts to bear which could be of enormous relevance for the strategic policy decisions on the future of the region. One important conclusion drawn by Ives and Messerli is that there are plural problem definitions and plural solution definitions and, more importantly, that they do not go away. If we insist on just one perception of the problem, then inevitably we will be excluding many of the people and, in the process, committing investment to a development path that, sooner or later, will prove unsustainable—physically, socially, or both. "Single problem/single solution" approaches (which again, are prevalent at present) inevitably foster wrong thinking. Right thinking requires us to develop, and strengthen "multiple problem/multiple solution" approaches.

The researchers advocate a broader, more holistic critical approach and an increased focus on the social, economic, institutional and political situation in which the region finds itself. This enables us to perceive mountain development as one side of the same coin of which environmental protection is the other. And it enables us to understand that—in the words of our researchers—"if the subsistence farmer is hungry, environment and culture become remote considerations "and unrealistic concepts". This is the Himalayan dilemma.

Edith Brown Weiss takes a different approach in her work on international law, common patrimony and intergenerational equity.[3] Brown Weiss' research also deals with complexity, the more complicated and dangerous challenges facing the international legal order as a consequence of accelerated technological changes and a growing sense of disjunction between territorial authority and the global scale of ecological stability.

Concern about the effect of current policies on the preservation of future life prospects prompted the development of this project with a view to studying the intertemporal dimension of international law, the responsibilities of future generations with regard to the natural environment and the norms required to fulfil them. Traditionally, only areas not subject to national jurisdiction such as outer space and the oceans have been considered as "global commons". The intergenerational perspective, which considers the planet as a "global commons" or "common patrimony" shared by all generations, changes the scope of international law to a much broader framework.

The natural and cultural systems are, therefore, inter-connected and any changes affecting one of the components will have repercussions not only on the present systems but also on future generations. In other words, while a State has sovereignty over its own territory, including the right to use and benefit from its resources, it also has an obligation to preserve that territory for future generations. It is crucial, therefore, to develop international norms to prevent harm, since the damage to future generations might prove irreversible with no chance of compensation for it. In her conclusion, Brown Weiss states that as we confront the fact that we exist only in relationship to generations that went before us and those that will come after, we must develop a planetary ethos which recognizes that we share the planet with all communities throughout time. We must recognize that there is a planetary trust by which we are all bound, which gives us certain planetary rights and obligations. We need to translate these into enforceable norms locally, nationally, and internationally, so that we may achieve intergenerational equity.

Linking technology and ecology for sustainability

There are two concepts leading in one direction: the utilization of environmentally sound technologies and the conservation of the ecological balance. In a comprehensive context, both are part of the multiple solution approaches necessary to guarantee a sustainable development. "To sustain" means, in its very basic definition "to keep alive". Sustainability represents the fairness to future generations. The concept of sustainable development derives from the fact that our current policies and trends are not likely to keep our planet alive. Such a concept would imply long-term ecological thinking and planning as well as projecting future needs. The importance of long-term planning must also be understood by decision-makers who are accustomed to short-term responses to emergencies rather than to forward-looking strategies. This concept has yet another vital aspect: "Sustainability", which draws the line between local development and the global environment, involves people and their needs and living conditions. It relates to rural migration as much as to urban development and hazardous waste in the developed world as much as deforestation in the developing world. It recognizes the interdependence between the two, and makes us aware of the linkages between the world's economics, technology and ecology.

Ignacy Sachs identifies five areas of "sustainability": social, economic, ecological, geographical and cultural sustainability. In the holistic and multiple-solution approaches pursued by the UNU, all of these areas have to be considered. Sachs calls for a new industrialization pattern, including the institutional capacity to steer such a process.

Economic restructuring requires detailed information and analysis of economic structures and their nexus with environmental variables. All countries will need to devote more attention and research efforts to this question. This should be supplemented by an analysis of the processes and instruments by which economic activity and environmental degradation can be effectively delinked. Furthermore, care must be taken to prevent the relocation of highly polluting industries in developing countries, in the process. The objective is to introduce through our network of researchers new ideas into the global discussion, and to question old ones. The concept of "creating learning" allows different and sometimes conflicting information to be considered in the decision-making process. In this process, one deals with a large degree of uncertainty and complexity and that there are no simple solutions. However, the results of such research on technology and ecology have made a significant contribution to a better understanding of the policy implications and the interlinkages between the two. It is now up to the political decision-makers at the international, regional and national levels to avail themselves of research results already available.

Notes

1. Deutsch, Karl W.: *The Nerves of Government,* Free Press, New York, 1965.

2. Ives, Jack D. and Messerli, Bruno: *The Himalayan Dilemma: Reconciling Development and Conservation,* Routledge/UNU, London, 1989.

3. Brown Weiss, Edith: *In Fairness to Future Generations. International Law, Common Patrimony, and Intergenerational Equity,* Transnational Publishers/UNU, New York, 1989.

Chapter 12

THE GLOBALIZATION OF FINANCE: DEBT-FOR-NATURE AND DEBT-FOR-SCHOLARS SWAPS

Susan Hagerty,* Tammy Warner, and Gligor Tashkovich

A s a result of the enormous burden of debt shouldered by developing countries, banks which originally issued that debt have become receptive to innovative ideas for relieving themselves of it. This paper aims to discuss debt-for-nature and debt-for-scholars swaps as realistic alternatives to using traditional financing for development activities. These possible strategies are elaborated using the successful experiences in the countries of Bolivia, Madagascar, Sudan and Ecuador.

Globalization of markets

It is likely that a global common market will replace politics and idealism as the driving force within the next decade. Ultimately, local governments will run the increasing risk of abdicating the fate of their commu-

*Managing Director, Hagerty Group, Inc., New York; former Vice-President, Shearson/American Express. The author is grateful to Tammy Warner and Gligor Tashkovich, graduate students in the Johnson School of Business, Cornell University, for their assistance in the preparation of this paper.

nities to transnational corporations. Adam-Smithian competition will not necessarily serve the best interests of those communities because transnational corporations rarely have any internal motivation to develop or preserve the natural and human resources of their host countries. At the same time, conservation groups worldwide, the United States Agency for International Development (USAID), banks, and a few select universities are working towards the creation of economically rational options which will preserve endangered habitats and encourage the intellectual development of human resources from those countries.

Ecological degradation

The overwhelming majority of biological species occur in the developing world. Tropical plants and animals, most of which have never even been catalogued, are disappearing at an increasing rate, swept away by a highly intrusive global economy which is not governed by any transnational political authority. Human resources and native traditions are similarly endangered as indigenous peoples find it impossible to sustain their modest ways of life. Alarmed at this trend, various conservation groups have begun to pressure the governments of these countries to slow the pace of ecological degradation. The nations who can least afford it have been charged with the responsibility of preserving their natural habitats for the good of the global community, without adequate incentives or compensation for their efforts.

Debt-for-nature swaps

Traditionally, developing countries have borrowed money to finance environmentally damaging projects, and the pressing need for hard currency to service this debt causes much of the additional deforestation within these nations. It is estimated that 11.3 million hectares of tropical forests disappear annually. Also, in recent years, least developed countries (LDCs) have been paying out for more in debt service that they have been receiving in development aid. Recently, conservation groups such as the World Wildlife Fund have realized that one solution to the ecological problems faced by developing countries may come through economic means. Examples of novel approaches to servicing developing country debt include so-called debt-for-nature swaps.

The concept of a debt-for-nature swap is fairly straight forward. With the administrative help of private financial institutions, LDC debt is purchased, generally at a maximum of 30 cents on the United States dollar. The purchasers may be either a developed country conservation group, the debtor government, or local conservation groups of the debtor nation. These various entities raise money to buy the debt through government funding, bank donations, or the generosity of individuals. The next step is to convert this purchased debt into the local currency equivalent. These funds are then either used directly for certain environmentally sound projects or else income-generating bonds are purchased whose proceeds are then used in the same way. As of April 1990, about $200 million in debt has been retired through these mechanisms.

For example, in Bolivia, it is estimated that 80 acres of tropical forest are lost every minute. Four years ago, banks sold $650,000 of Bolivian debt for $100,000 to Conservation International, which, in turn, had the Bolivian Government purchase four million acres of land (at an average cost of two cents an acre) to serve as a buffer around an already existing national park. Conservation International specializes in these types of swaps.

Similarly, the American branch of the World Wildlife Fund, with the blessing of the Government of Madagascar, purchased $2.1 million dollars (over half of its $3.5 million dollar debt) of the debt of Madagascar for $995,000—45 per cent of the face value of the debt. When it was converted, the local currency was spent on a variety of conservation projects—one of which included jobs for an additional four hundred park rangers. In this case, the money was provided by a one million dollar grant from USAID. USAID saw this as a good investment because over 165,000 plant and animal species exist only in Madagascar. This situation is due to the historical uniqueness and the relative inaccessibility of the island nation. These swaps, then, provide synergistic benefits to all the parties concerned: the banks, the debtor nations, the wildlife, and the people who become employed.

There are several options available for financing these types of conservation measures. In Bolivia's case, the local government has the responsibility of maintaining and expanding an existing national park, out of an operating fund provided in exchange for the debt. In a similar swap in Ecuador, the Government issued bonds in local currency. Interest from the bonds endows the Fundación Natura, a local conservation group that administers the national parks budget.

Before these debt-for-nature swaps can be fully utilized, the concerns of the financial institutions involved must be addressed. At this time, there are not many tax or other incentives for United States banks to donate the debt outright, although the situation is somewhat more favourable in certain European countries, such as the United Kingdom.

In December 1988, the Midland Bank handed over its total loan exposure in Sudan (amounting to $800,000) to the United Nations Children's Fund (UNICEF), which simultaneously arranged for the Sudanese Government to service them in local currency. The funds are being invested solely in water, sanitation, reforestation, and health education programmes in the Kordofan region of Sudan, and are administered by UNICEF. UNICEF assumes accountability for the use of the funds. The Sudanese Government has cooperated fully with UNICEF to establish the programme and is collaborating with UNICEF to implement it.

This leads to a situation in which cash sales have been the preferred mechanism. Some banks have been willing to donate the cash required for purchase. In order to provide an incentive for this type of transaction, banks need to have a continuing interest in the debtor country. In this way, the banks profit from the long-term development benefits enjoyed by the debtor nation. At present, the banks do at least have the motivation of saving the administrative costs involved with debt rescheduling. Finally, the debt-for-nature swaps create great goodwill and provide an enhanced image in all the markets of a participating bank.

Debt-for-scholars swaps

Harvard University offered to relieve banks holding Ecuadorian debt at an 85 per cent discount. Because the banks did not believe that they would ever be repaid by Ecuador, they were happy to sell the bonds at 15 per cent of their face value. Harvard invested $750,000 and subsequently bought $5 million of Ecuadorian debt. The Ecuadorian Government, in turn, established the Fundación Capacitar as a organizational vehicle through which Harvard returned the accumulated debt. In exchange, the Government gave the Foundation entirely new "stabilization bonds", with a new face value equal to half the face value of the retired debt. The Fundación Ecuador plans to convert 85 per cent of the money into United States dollars and use it to finance the study of Ecuadorian nationals at Harvard. The rest of the money will be used to support researchers from Harvard working in Ecuador over an agreed upon period of time.

Here is how all the participating organizations win. The banks can write off the loss associated with not receiving the full face value of the debt and are relieved of a significant burden with which they had otherwise planned to manage uncomfortably for the foreseeable future.

For its initial investment of $750,000, Harvard will realize revenue of $2.125 million or a profit of $1.375 million in tuition payments. It also establishes a close ongoing relationship with a country that has great future development potential, in, for example, the form of exchange, research, and programmes abroad.

Ecuador ends up with half as much outstanding debt, which reduces interest payments. The country also establishes a long-term relationship with a world-class university, which will eventually educate its future leaders. When these students return home, a domino effect is produced, because by implementing concepts learned abroad, they are effectively building their homeland for a new tomorrow.

Conclusions

So far, LDC debt has been sold at an extremely steep discount, reflecting the nearly insolvent nature of the nations involved. Obviously, issues of pricing are very important for conservation groups which rely on donations not only for their support but also to implement these environmentally sound strategies successfully in LDC countries. However, ecological damage and related indebtedness is not confined to small economies. In the case of larger, more solvent economies, the higher value of the debt creates greater difficulty in obtaining this type of financing.

Also, many developing countries, particularly in Central and South America, are extremely sensitive to foreign influence and the possibility of United States imperialism. The Bolivian press voiced serious concerns about the possibility of foreign control of national land. In this regard, the relationship of the local conservation group to that of the developed country is a vitally important variable. The conservation organizations of the developed country must exercise caution and avoid even the appearance of excessive influence over the projects.

Another consideration should be that of public perception within the LDC, particularly in regard to the consent of indigenous people who will be affected by ecological programmes. Not everyone will agree on what constitutes sustainability in development, and the more developed countries should be encouraging the democratic process in this context.

Finally, the issue of the long-term viability of these projects needs to be addressed. What are the guarantees, for example, that these projects will continue under unstable political conditions? Development and ecological safety will continue to be a matter of concern. Eastern Europe also has a tremendous debt problem, and perhaps these measures can be used to alleviate that problem as well.

With increasing realization of the connections between Third-World debt and environmental destruction, the role of multinationals that can break the debt service/deforestation cycle will increase. Competitive advantage will come as a result of ecologically sustainable development and the highest returns on investment will be for those projects that create positive externalities. As these programmes become more common and easier to administer, the best way for the global corporation to earn goodwill and ultimately increase market share and return on equity in developing countries will be by protecting and preserving their human and natural resources.

Chapter 13

INDUSTRIAL RESTRUCTURING FOR SUSTAINABLE DEVELOPMENT: THREE POINTS OF DEPARTURE

Udo E. Simonis*

At a forum on industry and the environment held in New Delhi, Stephan Paulus gave the following definition of ecological modernization: "Ecological modernization focuses on prevention, on innovation and structural change towards ecologically sound industrial development . . . It relies on clean technology, recycling, and renewable resources . . . To introduce such a concept into the economy, it is necessary to coordinate various policy areas, such as industrial, fiscal, energy, transport and environmental policies".

This, actually, is a rather broad and demanding definition of a concept proposed to achieve better harmony between economy and ecology. In this article I will, therefore, concentrate on only some aspects of such a concept. First, I am going to present some empirical evidence on the relationship between economic structure and environmental impacts; second, I shall point to some of the deficiencies of environmental policy, and third, I shall put forward some ideas on how to integrate ecological dimensions into economic policy.

*Director of the International Institute for Environment and Society, Berlin.

I
ECOLOGICAL STRUCTURAL CHANGE OF THE ECONOMY

In both the East and the West, economists, planners and engineers are seeking a solution to the problem of how to change the traditional patterns of resource use. "Perestroika" and "modernization" are two current catchwords in this process, and new environmental priorities play a part in the envisaged conversion of the economy. Harmonizing ecology and economy in a specific sense relies on the premise that a reduction in the resource input of production (ecological structural change) will lead to an *ex ante* reduction of emissions and wastes that have a negative impact on the natural environment (ecological structural change).

In order to clarify the relationship between economic structure, structural change, and environmental impacts, one needs suitable information concerning the material side of production, for environmental protection and resource conservation by the economy—and thus its long-term sustainability—cannot appropriately be described in such terms as income, investments and consumption. One possibility is to select and compare some indicators describing the environmentally relevant features of the production process. The availability of environmental indicators such as emission data relating to "representative" pollutants—for example, sulphur dioxide and nitrogen oxide—has grown recently (see the annual reports on the environment of several industrial nations, and those by the United Nations Environment Programme (UNEP) and the Organization for Economic Cooperation and Development (OECD). These indicators concern certain negative environmental effects of production. Less is known on the environmental relevance of the input factors in industrial production or on the question of which indicators provide environmentally significant information about the structure of the economy. Given the present state of statistics, only a few such indicators can be tested in a cross-national comparison of Eastern and Western countries.

De-linking economic growth
from environmentally relevant inputs

Using a set of four indicators (input factors), Jänicke et al. have studied 31 countries of both the Organization for International Economic Cooperation and the Organisation for Economic Cooperation for Development with regard to the relationship between economic structure and environmental impacts. The four factors whose direct and indirect environmental significance is thought to be self-evident were: energy, steel, cement, and freight transport. Regarding their patterns of production and consumption these are environmentally "hard" factors, characteristic of a certain structure of the economy and/or stage of economic development.

The main hypothesis of the research was a simple one and reads thus: positive environmental effects in structural change in the economy are to be expected by actively de-linking economic growth from the use of environmentally relevant inputs (resources). Such active de-linking (or ecological structural policy) would:

(a) Result in a decrease of resource depletion and/or environmental pollution;

(b) Mean *ex ante* instead of *ex post* environmental protection;

(c) Promote those integrated technologies which touch upon several environmental effects (pollutants) at one and the same time.

Structural change as a shift of input factors to more intelligent uses can thus be conceived as a process of successive de-linking. The contribution of traditional (hard) input factors to the national product decreases, that is, they change or lose their function in the development process.

Examples of successful and deficient de-linking

Taking Germany as an example, Jänicke has demonstrated a fivefold de-linking from the growth of the gross domestic product (GDP). The de-linking of energy and cement consumption and weight of freight transport from the GDP became apparent during the 1970s; regarding steel, the de-linking process had already begun in the 1960s. In this way, the structural change of the economy generated environmental gratis effects of various kinds:

(a) The stagnating consumption of primary energy led to a reduction of harmful emissions (pollutants);

(b) The relative decline in the weight of freight transport indicates that the volume of materials employed was reduced rather than increased;

(c) The fall in the use of cement represents a direct gratis effect as far as the emissions from cement factories are concerned; this decrease coincided with the trend towards the labour-intensive renovation of the housing stock, as compared to new construction;

(d) The decrease in steel consumption accounts for a considerable reduction in harmful emissions as far as processing is concerned; this drop was strongly marked and partly due to increased recycling activities.

Environmental gratis effects occur when the rate of usage of the input factors (resources) having a (strong) negative impact on the environment remains below the growth rate of the GDP. Comparing the rates of usage of the four selected input factors with the growth rate of the GDP, Jänicke et al. discovered three different development patterns:

(a) The factors having impacts on the environment decline absolutely; i.e., absolute structural improvements are induced, corresponding to absolute environmental gratis effects;

(b) The factors having impacts on the environment remain constant, or increase, but with a lower growth rate than the GDP; i.e., relative structural improvements, corresponding to relative environmental gratis effects;

(c) The factors having impacts on the environment increase at a higher growth rate than the GDP; i.e., structural deterioration occurs, corresponding to absolute negative environmental effects of economic growth.

In table 1, 16 out of the 31 countries studied are grouped according to these three development patterns.

TABLE 1

ENVIRONMENTAL IMPACTS DERIVING FROM STRUCTURAL CHANGE, PERCENTAGE CHANGES 1970-1985

Country	Consumption on primary energy	Crude steel	Cement production	Weight of freight transport	GDP[a]
Group 1: Absolute structural improvement					
Belgium	7.1	−24.5	−17.6	−2.2	42.7
Denmark	−2.7	−45.6	−33.2	20.1	40.8
France	30.3	−34.8	−23.4	−14.5	51.6
Germany	13.4	−26.3	−32.8	4.4	38.4
Sweden	26.4	−37.9	−41.2	−21.4	32.7
United Kingdom	−2.3	−43.5	−28.7	−18.2	32.4
Group 2: Relative structural improvement					
Austria	32.1	−33.9	−6.0	21.3	54.3
Finland	39.6	14.8	−11.2	12.2	65.7
Japan	37.3	−2.3	27.4	7.5	90.2
Norway	51.1	−21.6	−40.3	34.7	87.5
Group 3: Structural deterioration					
Bulgaria	74.9	24.9	42.3	77.5	37.3
Czechoslovakia	31.5	22.5	37.3	62.9	33.9
Greece[b]	119.3	67.3	162.9	43.1	69.1
Portugal[b]	89.0	34.2	133.1	27.4	69.0
Soviet Union	76.3	33.4	36.0	70.2	47.7
Turkey	218.8	184.4	173.2	118.6	118.2

[a]Calculation of the gross domestic product percentage changes on the basis of constant (1980) United States dollars. Bulgaria, Czechoslovakia and Soviet Union data refer to percentage changes 1970–1983 of the gross national product.
[b]Transport data only take railway transport data into account.
Source: Jänicke et al.

Of all the industrialized countries investigated by Jänicke et al., Sweden went through the most rapid structural change. The drastic reduction in cement production (– 41 per cent), the decreasing use of crude steel (– 38 per cent), and the decrease in the weight of freight transport (– 21 per cent) add up to notable environmental gratis effects or "absolute structural improvement".

In Japan, the de-linking process was partly neutralized by the rapid growth in industrial production and thus resulted only in "relative structural improvement".

In Czechoslovakia, no significant de-linking of economic growth from the four input factors took place. The development profile of this country, with sluggish structural change, is to some extent representative of the other economies of Eastern Europe.

Trends towards industrial restructuring

Despite certain analytical limitations of such empirical research (as, for example, the selection of only four input factors), several conclusions can be drawn from this international comparison as regards the trends of industrial restructuring:

(a) Structural change in the form of de-linking economic growth from environmentally relevant inputs was evident in most, but not all, the countries studied;

(b) Several countries enjoyed environmental gratis effects as a result of active structural change. In some cases, especially Sweden, these effects were quite considerable;

(c) In other countries, the possibly beneficial environmental effects of structural change were levelled off by the rapid industrial growth pursued. This was especially true for Japan;

(d) The strong correlation between the level of production (GDP) and environmental impacts, still evident in the 1970s, had dissolved in the 1980s. The high-income countries featured fairly rapid structural change;

(e) In the medium-income countries, a distinct pattern emerged in that there were cases of rapid quantitative growth and cases of qualitative growth, i.e., economic growth with constant or decreasing resource input.

All in all, it is therefore not yet possible to speak of one dominant trend towards industrial restructuring. However, the environmental gratis effects of active structural change are highly evident and thus provide one strategic element of the ecological modernization of industrial society.

I I
PREVENTIVE ENVIRONMENTAL POLICY

Theoretically speaking, environmental policy may be defined as the sum of objectives and measures designed to regulate society's interaction with the environment as a natural system; it comprises aspects of rehabilitation, conservation, and structural adjustment. Practice, however, does not conform to such a broad definition. Only parts of the interaction between society and environment become the subject of policy. So far, environmental policy has been designed mostly as react-and-cure strategies concerning air and water pollution, noise, and waste, with emphasis on the rehabilitation aspect.

For a variety of reasons, this conventional environmental policy was, and still is, meaningful and very necessary. It has, however, a number of deficits, some of which are cited in the following, along with some suggestions for overcoming them through preventive environmental policy, i.e., anticipate-and-prevent strategies.

Environmental expenditures and environmental damages

Since the beginning of the 1970s, when systematic records first began to keep track of the funds allocated for environmental protection, the sum of the respective public and private investments has reached large proportions in the industrialized countries. Industrial society thus appears to be paying very heavily in the form of back payments for the negative environmental costs of production accumulated in the past.

In Germany, for instance, this sum has risen to about $140 billion. In a detailed study, Leipert et al., from the International Institute for Environment and Society (IIES), have computed and classified all existing data on investments and expenditures aimed at repairing and protecting the environment.

Table 2 shows the total and sectoral environmental protection investments for the manufacturing sector of the German economy for the years 1975 to 1985.

Table 3 shows the total costs of environmental protection (current expenditures and depreciations) for both industry and government for the years 1975 to 1985.

Figures such as these are, however, ambivalent. On the one hand, they give cause for proud political statements about the successes of environmental protection, according to the motto "the more, the better". On the other hand, they are—presumably—the absolute minimum of what is necessary to secure the very basis for society's sustainability. At the same time, they symbolize a serious structural deficit of industrial society. Environmental protection expenditures are spent when damage to the natural environment has occurred and can no longer be denied. Belated, they are repairs to the process of economic growth, signs of a "post-fact" policy that reacts to damages (and must react to them) but does not, or cannot, prevent them. Therefore, it is necessary to confront the success stories of environmental protection expenditures with figures on the environmental damages themselves.

Again taking Germany as an example, a recent estimation by Lutz Wicke from the Federal Environmental Protection Agency, showed that the annual damage to the natural environment is above 103 billion deutschmarks, or in the order of 6 per cent of GNP, and not 3 per cent, as the OECD had estimated for the industrialized countries some years ago.

TABLE 2
ENVIRONMENTAL PROTECTION INVESTMENTS, MANUFACTURING SECTOR, FEDERAL REPUBLIC OF GERMANY, 1975–1985

Year	Total investments		Waste disposal		Water pollution control		Noise abatement		Air pollution control	
	Current prices	1980 prices	Current prices	1980 prices	Current prices	1980 prices	Current prices	1980 prices	Current prices	1980 prices
In millions of DM										
1975	2,480	3,090	170	210	900	1,110	200	240	1,210	1,530
1976	2,390	2,830	200	230	820	960	220	260	1,150	1,380
1977	2,250	2,560	200	230	740	850	210	230	1,100	1,250
1978	2,150	2,370	170	180	680	750	200	220	1,100	1,220
1979	2,080	2,190	260	160	760	800	200	210	960	1,020
1980	2,650	2,650	210	210	910	910	240	240	1,290	1,290
1981	2,940	2,810	250	240	950	910	210	200	1,530	1,460
1982	3,560	3,250	390	360	1,130	1,030	230	210	1,810	1,650
1983	3,690	3,270	290	260	1,100	990	230	200	2,070	1,820
1984	3,500	3,100	270	240	1,040	920	230	190	1,960	1,750
1985	5,620	4,940	330	280	1,060	910	260	220	3,970	3,530
Average annual change in percentage										
1975/84	+ 3.9	– 0.0	+ 5.3	+ 1.5	+ 1.6	– 2.1	+ 1.6	– 2.6	+ 5.5	+ 1.5
1975/79	– 4.3	– 8.2	– 1.5	– 6.6	– 4.1	– 7.9	0.0	– 3.3	– 5.6	– 9.6
1979/84	+ 11.0	+ 7.2	+ 11.0	+ 8.4	+ 6.5	+ 2.8	+ 2.8	– 2.0	+ 15.3	+ 11.4

Source: IIES research project.

– 176 –

TABLE 3
TOTAL COSTS OF ENVIRONMENTAL PROTECTION, FEDERAL REPUBLIC OF GERMANY, IN MILLIONS OF DM
1975–1985

Year	Industry			Government			Industry and Government		
	Current expenditures	Depreciation	Total costs	Current expenditures	Depreciation	Total costs	Current expenditures	Depreciation	Total costs
At current prices									
1975	3,200	1,520	4,720	3,000	1,920	4,920	6,200	3,440	9,640
1980	5,160	2,250	7,410	4,690	3,390	8,080	9,850	5,640	15,490
1985	7,930	3,160	11,090	6,430	4,340	10,770	14,360	7,500	21,860
At 1980 prices									
1975	4,050	1,870	5,920	3,790	2,570	6,360	7,840	4,440	12,280
1980	5,160	2,250	7,410	4,690	3,390	8,080	9,850	5,640	15,490
1985	6,230	2,640	8,870	5,340	4,030	9,370	11,570	6,670	18,240

Source: IIES research project.

Table 4 is based on different estimation methods, using data on actual damage costs and findings from willingness-to-pay studies. Although the results must be taken with some care, the table illustrates that despite high annual environmental protection expenditures, enormously high environmental damages still occur annually. Of course, this situation may be true not only for Germany but for many other countries as well.

There are more shortcomings of conventional environmental policy. Environmental policy usually identifies the given problem too late, so that the ecosystems affected cannot survive. As it is pursued as a media-specific policy, i.e., separately regulating air and water quality, noise or waste, it also runs the risk of lacking coordination between its specific goals, measures and institutions. And this may then result in shifting a problem from one environmental medium to another, for example, from air to water or soil, or from one place to another, as is the case with long-range, trans-boundary pollution. In addition,

TABLE 4
ENVIRONMENTAL DAMAGE IN
THE FEDERAL REPUBLIC OF GERMANY
("Measurable damage" in billions of DM per year)

Environmental sectors	Environmental damage
Air pollution	ca. 48.0
Health hazards	2.3–5.8
Material damage	2.3+
Degradation of vegetation	1.0+
Forest blight, etc.	5.5–8.8
Water pollution	17.6++
Damage to rivers and lakes	14.3+
Damage to the North Sea and Baltic Sea	0.3++
Contamination of ground water, etc.	3.0+
Soil contamination	5.2++
Cost of Chernobyl disaster	2.4+
Rehabilitation of "yesterday's waste"	1.7
Cost of preserving biotopes and species	1.0+
Other soil contamination, etc.	0.1++
Noise	32.7+
Degradation of residential amenities	29.3+
Productivity losses	3.0+
"Noise rents," etc.	0.4+
Grand total of damage	103.5

Source: Wicke.

environmental policy often becomes entangled in a debate on principles. If measures must be taken quickly, the argument gets shifted from the "polluter-pays-principle"—which is advocated in general—to the "taxpayer-pays-principle", thereby switching the burden of environmental protection from the individual polluter to the community, to government or to society at large.

Thus, innovations in planning and implementation are needed. Preventive environmental policy—it seems—can counter the shortcomings of conventional environmental policy. In order to switch to preventive policy, however, several conceptual as well as practical constraints must be overcome.

One constraint has to do with the particular history of an environmental impact. In cases of yesterday's wastes, when damage has already occurred, a curative strategy is probably the only conceivable option. In cases where no damage has occurred as yet but where damage is expected for the future, the choice between a preventive and a curative strategy is basically open. In such a situation, the anticipatory principle leads to encourage the first option. As practice often is a mixture between the existing and the new, most policies actually will also include a mixture of prevention and cure. Demanding preventive environmental policy will then mean seeking and at last finding a better balance between the anticipatory and the reactive component within the policy action.

Basic conditions for preventive environmental policy

According to Scimemi and Winsemius, one can conceive three factors as concomitant policy-relevant processes in time: the accumulation of environmental damage; the acquisition of technical knowledge; and the rise of public awareness. The time sequence of these processes, especially the relative timing of their critical level, is decisive for the whole issue of preventive environmental policy.

To illustrate the relationship between these three factors, Scimemi has redrawn a diagram suggested by Winsemius, using three separate functions: level of damage; level of technical knowledge; and level of public awareness. The relative position and the shape of these functions depends, of course, on the specific circumstances i.e., country, environmental sector, and historical phase under consideration. The accumulation of damage starts at a given point in history when neither the scientific community nor the general public is yet aware that anything of importance is happening. The process of gathering technical knowledge may not start until some time after damage has begun to accumulate and proceeds gradually. During that phase, the public may still be unaware of the hazard. It is only some time later that public awareness starts to rise.

Within these concomitant processes, a certain stage becomes important: the technical understanding of the issue reaches a critical level, thus ensuring the first of two conditions required for effective policy action, i.e., technical rationality. Public awareness also reaches a critical level at which the second condition for effective decision-making, i. e., political viability, is fulfilled. It is at this stage that action will be undertaken to avoid the occurrence of further damage.

Recalling past developments in environmental policy at the national or the international level, it is easy to recognize that the processes evolved very much in conformity with Scimemi's theoretical interpretation.

What are now the opportunities to influence these basic conditions of policy action in favour of preventive environmental policy? Three general and two specific options emerge. The general options are: (a) retarding damage accumulation; (b) accelerating technical knowledge; and (c) increasing public awareness. The specific options are: (a) dynamic environmental standard-setting; and (b) dynamic public participation. All these various options make policy decisions possible at a stage when the level of environmental damage is still relatively low.

Environmental impact assessment as part of preventive policy

Acceleration of knowledge and awareness can, of course, be promoted through a variety of approaches and methods and depends a great deal on the specific environmental issue at hand. Environmental impact assessments (EIA) are increasingly being applied, not only for public but also for private investment projects. They entail efforts to learn more about possible environmental impacts and are intended to allow appropriate action to be taken before damage has occurred. In that sense, environmental impact assessments can be classified as part and parcel of preventive environmental policy.

During the last years, some headway has been made to institutionalize and standardize EIA procedures, nationally and, to a minor extent, internationally. As the EIA procedure is used particularly for specific investment projects, it allows for the "accelerating effort" to be targeted and generally also permits the burden of such efforts to be imposed upon the project initiator himself, thus conforming to a pre-condition of preventive environmental policy, i.e., the polluter-pays-principle. A big deficit, however, remains in how to implement EIA as a preventive procedure in cases of global change, such as climate warming or ocean pollution.

The required levels regarding technical knowledge and/or public participation in environmental decision-making differ widely from one environmental medium and country to the other. The question of how much knowledge and awareness is enough normally falls upon the political decision-maker i. e., the government, the environmental protection agency, the institution in charge of the problem, even if the scientific community, or parts of it, is ready to say "we know enough" and the public, or parts of it is demanding "something must be done". Therefore, stalemates in decision-making on environmental issues are quite frequent.

What constitutes enough knowledge or awareness for one country, government or institution, may not be enough for another. The normal outcome of such a situation is a compromise over the emission standards to be implemented. They will be weaker than technically or politically feasible because knowledge and awareness on cause-effect relationships or social priorities is said to be insufficient. Eminent cases in point are the emission standards for sulphur dioxide and nitrogen oxide in air pollution and the nitrate standard in water pollution. Thus, the dilemma of setting stricter emission standards is serious. Meanwhile, the forests may continue to die back, the ozone layer may continue to be affected, and water may continue to become contaminated.

The conclusion, therefore, is that environmental standard-setting must be conceived as a continuous process. With growing knowledge and awareness on actual and probable environmental damage the thresholds for action must be consecutively lowered, i.e., standard-setting must be dynamized so that industrial restructuring can be achieved quickly.

This need to come to terms with the future is not unique to environmental policy, as Scimemi rightly observed. Implementing the prevention principle is especially requested in all other domains of policy where collective interests are at stake. One such major domain we have to address when discussing the possibilities and impediments of ecological modernization is, of course, economic policy.

III
ECOLOGY AND ECONOMIC POLICY

Conflicts between economy and ecology

C.F. von Weizsäcker has said that ecology in essence means the necessary and feasible harmony between man and nature, society and environment. In general, however, economy means disharmony with nature. Use is made of nature both directly and indirectly when raw materials are processed into products, and nature is polluted by the emissions and wastes generated by industrial production. These are, then, the two processes in which nature remains the loser: natural raw materials are exchanged for produced waste materials. Besides labour and capital, nature is the truly quiescent and exploited third production factor. How, then, can nature's position in the "economy game" be strengthened?

The use of raw materials and the generation of emissions and wastes are of course, old, not new, issues. Scientific and technological development, however, has made it possible to increase the exploitation of the depletable resources, and has led to an ever-increasing accumulation of harmful emissions and non-decomposable wastes. Nature is no longer able to absorb all of these substances, many of which are not only toxic for flora and fauna but for human beings as well.

Efforts to hide harmful emissions and toxic wastes in land-fill sites, in transfer stations or permanent depositions, to spread them through high smokestacks and incinerators, or to dump them into the water bodies and abroad have at best been temporarily successful because many emissions and wastes are "mobile poisons" or reappear in different form. These activities lead to what Johan Galtung called the "linearization of ecological cycles," i. e., the natural diversity is reduced, the robustness of ecosystems declines and ecological symbioses and equilibria break down. As a consequence, environmental degradation increases and the absorption capacity of the natural environment decreases.

Accordingly, the conflict between ecology and economy can be attributed to two basic principles that are actually or possibly incompatible: (a) the ecological principle of stability, as a precondition for the sustainability of ecological systems; and (b) the economic principle of growth as the inherent logic of economic systems—more precisely, the principles of business profitability, national economic growth, and world market expansion.

Given the actual and the pending ecological crisis, the question arises as to whether these economic principles can be changed, reshaped and finally brought into harmony with ecological principles, and at which level, in what way, and at what time. It is, of course, a controversial question both in theory and in practice and presents a specific challenge to the social sciences. The answer depends not only upon the respective individual and societal constellation of interests. It depends particularly upon the ability of and the willingness for social innovations, i.e., on (a) whether the potential of an ecological self-regulation of the economy is used and (b) how the option of an ecological re-orientation of economic policy is implemented.

Ecological self-regulation of the economy

Let us start with a general statement. Most certainly, only a small fraction of the current environmental problems would exist (a) had the economic contexts remained so comprehensible that producers and consumers were personally able to recognize and be liable for the consequences of their own decisions towards depleting resources and polluting nature or (b) if business profitability, national economic growth, and the expansion of world markets could not be increased by externalizing parts of the ensuing costs. This is the old but still unresolved problem of the external effects of production. Scientific and technological development has been, and still is, coupled with negative external effects, i.e., the shifting of costs to society, future generations, and nature. With respect to the environmental problem, all these cost components are relevant. Let us take, as an example, acid rain and the ensuing damage to the forests.

First, the example of acid rain shows that a part of the costs of industrial production, i.e., the adequate reduction of air pollutants has been shifted to nature, which is resistant only up to a certain level: the forests are dying. Secondly, this example shows the shifting of costs onto succeeding generations, bequeathing a future with less or even no forests in some regions. Thirdly, this example shows the shifting of costs onto third parties (i.e., partial expropriation of the forest owners) and onto society, in the sense that economic and technical decisions of individual polluters (especially emissions from power plants, cars, transboundary pollution) impair the well-being and the physical health of the population.

Thus, the economic system evidently makes incorrect calculations with respect to the "ecosystem forest". Both business accounting and national accounting do not provide adequate signals to prevent pollution levels that are not tolerable for the ecological system. Conventional accounting shows favourable balances for the production of energy, for the automobile producers, and for the exporters of pollutants (just to stay with the three sources of pollution mentioned above), although the "ecosystem forest" is definitely being damaged by the emissions from these economic sectors. Losses here, profits there; compensation does not take place nor is liability provided for.

One of the pending tasks both for theory and practice can thus easily be prescribed. We should internalize the external effects of production, shift the costs back to the economic units that cause the environmental problem, and include the ecological perspective into all investment decision-making. Drastically reducing the external effects of production on society, nature, and future generations seems to be the necessary step towards regaining harmony between economy and ecology. But, how to proceed in practice and where to put priority?

To reorganize the economy towards a materially integrated cycle would, first of all, mean to reduce systematically the use of depletable resources and the generation of polluting emissions and wastes—and this is in contradiction to the prevailing "throughput economy" as seen by K. Boulding. In practice, recycling and clean technology are still at an incipient stage and not systematic economic undertakings. In particular, the step from simply disposing wastes towards avoiding wastes ("low waste economy") has not been made.

Certainly, this is in part because the recycling of many waste products is impossible or extremely costly. But it is also true because adequate price and cost signals have not been set. The prevention of waste generation and the conservation of depletable resources are still not being sufficiently promoted. This state of affairs, however, has also to do with the above-mentioned structural deficits of the economic accounting procedures, which do not adequately measure the diminishing stocks. Therefore, two contradictory trends can be observed: increasing monetary income and decreasing natural stock.

Proposals for ecological accounting at the factory level and in the national accounts, however, are promising. With ecological accounting, the amount of energy, materials, wastes, land use, etc., are being computed and, by simulating the given shortage, accounting units are determined and then enter the accounts. Thus, a measure is developed which not only may guide private investment decision-making, but at the same time will provide a public information instrument for promoting qualitative economic processes.

In industrial society, another ecological principle is no longer adhered to, that of the sustainability of resource use. Traditionally, forest owners, for instance, have followed the rule: do not cut down more wood than you regrow. This rule is being undermined: externally produced acid rain collides with internal resource conservation and accumulated external debt leads to the overexploitation of national resources. The goal of sustaining the yield of the forest capital stock is being undermined by indirect expropriation and resource depletion.

One basic principle to be re-established in the economy is that of responsibility or liability. With respect to environmental problems, the legal system and economic behaviour in most countries is marked by the strict proof of causality. Only when the injured party can prove who caused the damage is the polluter held liable for compensation. Instead, statistical probability is in some countries and in some cases sufficient to obligate industry to compensate for damages as a kind of collective liability. Once this principle was established by the courts and through legislation, it quickly helped to improve environmental quality through ecological self-regulation of business activities.

In general, the liability principle would strengthen the anticipate-and-prevent strategy in environmental policy, and shift the technical solutions for environmental problems from *ex post* to *ex ante* approaches, i.e., from controlling or end-of-pipe technology towards low emission or integrated technology. To implement the principle in practice, small steps or big leaps could be taken: from continuous reporting on wastes or automatic monitoring of emissions to collective funds and strict environmental liability.

Ecological reorientation of economic policy

Confronted with serious environmental damage, conventional economic policy is increasingly being challenged. Its guiding principles, goals, instruments, and institutions are being questioned, and a new concept is emerging: ecological economic policy.

Conventional economic policy is based on the guiding principle of maximizing flows: volume of production, income, profits, turnover— the throughput economy referred to above. Ecological economy, however, is based on a different guiding principle, i.e., increasing efficiency and maintaining substance. Aspects such as environmental compatibility and resource conservation become important; structural adjustment of products and technologies according to ecological considerations becomes the task.

Regarding goals, it seems necessary to redefine and supplement the conventional economic policy goals, especially to reassess the growth target and to include environmental stability into the catalogue of economic policy goals. The conventional policy goal indicators were developed at a time when environmental pollution was already a problem but not yet a public issue; they have not really been readjusted since. Economic growth is still being measured in terms of goods and income categories only (gross national product) while their effects on the stock and the quality of the resources (natural capital) are not adequately considered. In the conventional concept of economic growth, all monetary transactions are summed up independently of their specific function; also increasing expenditures are included that are spent solely for the necessary compensation for damage originally caused by the production process; in other words, compensatory or defensive expenditures.

Qualified goal indicators for economic policy can be defined in various ways: computations of compensatory expenditures, i.e., assessment of an environmentally related net product ("eco-national product"); combined growth and distribution indices (redistribution with growth); an integrated system of economic and environmental indicators, or an attached "satellite system".

Regarding instruments, conventional economic policy relies mainly on two instruments: variations of interest rates and variations of tax rates. From an ecological point of view, new taxes and charges are required which, to some extent, should replace traditional taxes. In a situation of structural unemployment and environmental pollution, the introduction of resource taxes such as an energy tax, emission charges on, for example, sulphur dioxide, nitrogen oxide and carbon dioxide emissions, and a definite decrease of wage taxes is called for. Such a structural tax reform would change the existing incentives in the economy towards the acceleration of resource efficiency and the increase of employment opportunities.

Economic policy manifests itself in and works through particular institutions. Therefore, an ecological orientation of economic policy also requires the creation of new institutions and the abolition or re-definition of old ones. The current debate on the negative environmental effects of decisions by the World Bank and the IMF are just a case in point. The actual and the pending environmental crisis require structural institutional reforms by which economic institutions would have to incorporate the ecological perspective. Environmental institutions would have to improve their competence and integrate assessments of environmental impact into all major economic decision-making.

Conclusion

According to these deliberations, industrial restructuring for sustainable development or "ecological modernization" is obviously a demanding concept, both methodologically and practically. Its implementation requires a far-reaching conversion of the economy, a reorientation of environmental policy, and a replenishment of economic policy. The three main strategic elements or points of departure seem to be ecological structural change of the economy; preventive environmental policy; and ecological orientation of economic policy. They reconcile the interests of man and nature, society and environment. The social sciences—economics, sociology, jurisprudence, political science, psychology—must develop further the methodological foundations and improve the institutional arrangements for a successful practical implementation of such a concept.

Chapter 14

A STRATEGY FOR DELIBERATE SOCIAL CHANGE IN CITIES

Janice E. Perlman*

For millennia, cities have been the centres of culture and the crucibles for the advance of civilization. But until recently the vast majority of the population has lived in tiny settlements, villages and small towns. As the year 2000 approaches, we find ourselves in the midst of four dramatic global transformations which force us to rethink the nature of human settlements.

Rural–urban

The world is becoming predominantly urban. In 1800, only 3 per cent of the world's population lived in urban areas; in 1950, it was 29 per cent, and shortly after the year 2000 over 50 per cent of the world's population will be living in cities.

North–South

While cities in the industrialized countries face stabilizing or even declining populations, urban population growth in developing countries is dramatic. Estimates predict that from 1950 to 2050 the urban population in Third World countries will have increased almost 16 times,

*Executive Director of the Megacities Project and Senior Research Scientist at New York University's Urban Research Center. This article appeared in a different form in *Cities*, February 1990. It has been edited by Üner Kirdar for this book.

from under 200 million to a total of 3150 million people. Given that urban population growth in developing countries is three times that of industrialized countries, by the year 2000 the urban population of developing countries will be almost twice that of developed nations and almost four times larger by the year 2025.

Formal–informal

This astonishing growth is not equally distributed throughout the urban fabric. About half is due to immigration from the countryside, and since the vast majority of these migrants do not have the resources to purchase or rent in the "formal" housing market, they live in squatter settlements, shanty towns, illegal subdivisions, or tenements in deteriorated and peripheral neighbourhoods. Thus, while the "formal city" may be growing at an average of 3–4 per cent per year, the "informal city" is growing at twice that rate.

Cities–megacities

Cities are reaching sizes unprecedented in human history. By the turn of the century, there will be 23 cities with populations of 10 million or more, as compared with only one 50 years ago. Eighteen of these will be in the developing countries. At that population scale, each of these cities will hold more people than some 100 United Nations member nations today.

The policy response

Surprisingly, the international donor community has been quite slow to respond. Current calculations by the International Institute for Environment and Development show that most aid agencies and development banks allocate less than 15 per cent of their funds to basic needs projects in urban areas, and less than 20 per cent to all other urban development projects. The focus of attention continues to be the rural peasant and agricultural policy rather than the city squatter and urban policy. Clearly, the two are closely interrelated, but the imbalance of attention is striking in light of the emerging realities.

Virtually every country has responded to the "urban explosion" by trying to limit the growth of their largest cities. These efforts range from restricting in-migration to dispersing the would-be migrants (to growth poles, new capitals, smaller cities, or resettlement areas) and to stimulating regional and rural development in hopes of equalizing the level of living in the countryside and the city.

These efforts have had limited success. Some, such as rural development, have proven counterproductive, actually hastening out-migration from the countryside. The fundamental reason for the failure of these policies is not only the lack of resources, enforcement mechanisms or political will, but also the fact that cityward migration benefits the individuals, families, communities of origin, cities, and the nation as a whole. Going against urbanization is going against the tide of national development, and all of the socioeconomic and political forces that spur that development.

The cityward migrants who are voting with their feet are intuitively correct. Not only is there more economic opportunity in the city, but the larger the city, the greater the opportunity. Empirical evidence also shows that large cities are more productive, and the largest cities are likely to be particularly more productive relative to others in a less developed country. These cities typically account for 80–85 per cent of their national GNP. Furthermore, detailed analyses of revenues and national budget expenditures show that funds and resources from central cities are transferred to, and benefit, the rest of the countries.

The challenge

This is not to say that megacities do not have severe problems. In fact, these problems are often so linked with city size and management capacity that in many ways Rio de Janeiro, Bombay, Shanghai, and New York City have more in common with each other than with the smaller cities and towns in their own countries. To begin with, the sheer size of the megacities presents a situation for which we have no collective experience. No precedent exists for feeding, sheltering or transporting so many people in so dense an area, nor for removing their waste products or providing clean drinking water. Urban systems based on human settlements of 50,000 or 250,000 may be able to accommodate urban populations of one million, but begin to break down at four million, and are blatantly unworkable at 10 million. What is needed is a more sophisticated and sensitive management capability than anything we have developed to date.

Exacerbating the problem, the megacities are experiencing critical environmental degradation, pushing to the limit their ability to sustain human life. While all urbanites are affected, the urban poor are the most vulnerable, since squatter settlements are often located in the most undesirable areas of the cities such as floodplains, steep hillsides, or adjacent to dangerous industries. Leonard and Petesch point out in their following article that environmental degradation now represents one of the most formidable constraints on productivity for the urban poor. It threatens the physical security of people and their possessions and increases opportunistic diseases that debilitate adults and kill infants. Innovative solutions that deal with automobile and industrial emissions, garbage and sewerage recycling, water and waste treatment, and detoxification in the megacities will go a long way to healing our environment and preserving "our global future".

However, the physical infrastructure of every city is based on the same fundamental systems which were invented a century ago in a brief 12-year span between 1877 and 1889, before ecological problems became an issue. As Eberhard explains, these include indoor plumbing, the incandescent lamp, the electric trolley, steel-frame buildings and elevators, the internal combustion engine, the subway, and the telephone. Most of these systems are incredibly costly to install and maintain, and unnecessarily wasteful of water, energy and materials. Over the past 100 years, the major advances in science and technology have been applied to the military and to consumer products. The question now is how to find creative ways to apply these advances to the building and maintenance of the urban infrastructure, and the preservation of the environment.

Thus, all megacities, regardless of demographic factors, level of economic development, political structure, or sociocultural background, share certain fundamental problems. These include increasing demands on limited city budgets, extreme polarization between rich and poor, severe environmental strain, fragmented programme initiatives, isolation among sectors and disciplines, and powerful resistance to change in the status quo. These problems are reinforced by incentive systems which discourage public policy risk-taking while encouraging them in private enterprise.

The opportunity

The timing is urgent. Experience has shown that there is often a 20–25 year time lag between new ideas and their incorporation into public policy. In the case of low-income housing policy, for example, it was recognized in the early 1960s that the self-built shanty towns of Third World cities were not the problem but the solution, and that giving land tenure to the squatters and providing urbanized lots in peripheral areas yielded better results than the bulldozer. Yet it took almost a generation for these ideas to be adopted, first by the international agencies (World Bank 1972), then by national governments (early 1980s) and now finally—and still only partially—by local governments.

We cannot afford to wait another generation for the next set of urban policy innovations to address the needs of city dwellers. Even if current birth control programmes and efforts to encourage the growth of small and intermediate-size cities are much more successful than those in the past, there will still be hundreds of millions of people living in the world's largest cities and more migrating there. Thus, it is time to turn our attention to how to make megacities work better for the people who are there and those who are inevitably coming.

So where can we find solutions to these problems? Conventional solutions are not the answer. Jorge Wilheim, the former Planning Director of São Paulo, has calculated that it would cost the present equivalent of 30 municipal annual budgets to make up the deficits in the physical and social infrastructure using traditional approaches. It is unlikely that such resources will be available in the foreseeable future. As Per Ljung explains, the $100–150 billion invested by developing countries annually in shelter and infrastructure falls far short of what is needed for adequate shelter and basic services, and foreign aid (which last year amounted to less than $4 billion) is not likely to fill the gap in the near future. To make matters worse, he argues that most institutions responsible for managing urban growth are weak, and with few exceptions, past government policies and programmes have tended to worsen urban problems rather than contribute to their solutions. Research institutes, consultants and academics are not the most fertile sources for answers. Experience over the past 20 years shows that, since intelligence is not distributed along class or geographic lines, the most promising innovative approaches often come from local experience— from the people, community groups, street-level bureaucrats, and small-scale enterprises closest to coping with problems on a daily basis.

Conclusions

There is enough energy and creativity in the cities today to address the challenges, but there are too few mechanisms to channel these forces into the policy-making process or to multiply the effects of approaches to that work. If decisions concerning service provision continue to be dominated by the public sector there is little possibility for local communities to spur innovations and experiments in non-public service delivery. There is thus a compelling need to discover alternative approaches that make better use of the abundant human and natural resources in the city and create multiplier effects with the scarce financial resources. We need to rethink or re-envision a city of the 21st century—one which is socially just, ecologically sustainable, politically participatory, and economically viable—not merely a projection of the 19th century city with all its negative connotations.

The bottom line is a concern for the well-being of the 322.56 million citizens of megacities in the year 2000, and with the way cities will work for all of their residents in the 21st century. If we are to turn around the sense of hopelessness and despair about these large urban agglomerations, what is required is not simply a set of interesting ideas that happen to work in one context, but the cumulative effect of these ideas in enabling us to rethink the cities of the future. Given the deeply vested interests in the status quo, how can we find the political will for urban transformation in a non-revolutionary situation? The management of city problems cannot be separated from wider issues—of income distribution both between social groups and between nations, the international economy, sustainable development, and human values.

Throughout history, cities have been the crucibles of culture and the source of major advances of civilization. The boldness of our quest for deliberate social change and the transformation of urban practices from the neighbourhood level all the way to city, national and international levels is at the heart of whether we continue to project 19th century solutions onto tomorrow's world, or finally make the leap to the 21st century city.

Chapter 15

WOMEN AND THE ENVIRONMENT

Emel Dogramaci*

Ultimately there is only one environment and we all have to share it. We also have to share responsibility for preserving it, and this is indeed a grave responsibility. Some people—because they are better equipped or better positioned—can be expected to contribute more towards the preservation of the environment, some less; but every single person can contribute something, and absolutely no one has the right to sit back and do nothing.

First, let us think about what we mean by the term "environment". It means, basically, the things surrounding us. These can be concrete, physical things like houses and shops or farm land and forests; or they can be human factors like luxury and poverty, freedom and restriction, ignorance and knowledge. Another important point is that there are no effective boundaries between one part of the environment and the next. Let us for a moment consider a garden, or rather a group of gardens. Each garden is owned by a family, and each family is free to do what it wants in its garden. But, one family, let us say, makes an awful lot of noise so neighbouring families cannot do what they want, that is, relax in peace and quiet. Another family leaves plastic bags and newspapers lying everywhere, and the wind comes and carries them over into other

*Dean of the Faculty of Letters, Hacettepe University, Ankara.

gardens, making them look like rubbish tips. One garden is left to grow wild and the wind carries the seeds of the weeds into neighbouring gardens where they grow fast in the well cultivated soil and start to compete with the good flowers. There are trees planted all round the edge of one garden, and the roots spread deep and wide and sap the goodness from the earth of neighbouring gardens. The point is that one garden cannot exist separately from the rest. In the same way, one country and one continent cannot exist separately from the rest. There is only one environment, and we have to share it. Now sharing is an attitude. It has to be taught, not only in the classroom but also in the home, and this is an area in which women can contribute a great deal to the protection of the environment.

A child has to learn, by example and suggestion, to share toys, to share space, to share pleasure, to share sorrow, to share duties. Sharing means being sensitive to other people's needs and moods. It means realizing that someone who is ill does not want noise, someone who is tired would appreciate a little help, someone who is lonely looks forward to a visit. People who thus learn to be considerate will not willingly increase the pollution of the world's environment, neither will people who have learned to respect and love all forms of nature, from plants and flowers and trees to butterflies and birds and tigers.

During the early years of a child's life, it is the mother who is in the best position to inculcate such attitudes. And this can be done in very simple ways. Plants and flowers around the house can help. So can mint and parsley growing in pots on the child's balcony. City children are too cut off from the sources of the food they eat. All they know is that as long as you have the money you can buy potatoes and peppers and pears. But ask them which of those three grows on a tree and you are likely to get some surprising answers. How different is the attitude of the child that has learned to appreciate the miracle of nature by watching, say, a bean on wet blotting paper swell, then split and send down a root and later throw up a green shoot. Such a child is much more likely to grow into an adult who naturally respects the environment.

Women should take young children to the city parks more often, and pressure the authorities for bigger and better ones. They might even put pressure on the schools to turn part of the playground into a play garden where the children can learn what it means to dig and plant and weed and water and watch things grow and finally reap a harvest.

It is also important for a child to become accustomed to a clean and tidy environment so that it becomes second nature for him to put rubbish in the bins where it belongs, not to leave litter around after a picnic and not to throw bottles into the sea. Here again, the influence of a mother or an aunt can be vital. These may seem like small things, but, as the Turkish saying has it: "From many drops of water you get a lake".

Let us consider another aspect of waste disposal: recycling. This practice has unfortunately not yet been taken up very widely in Turkey, but here again mothers, in cooperation with the schools, could help to inculcate recycling habits. Silver paper is an obvious example. It would be a simple matter for children to collect it from friends and neighbours and take it to school. Classes could compete for the biggest collection, and at the end of each term the silver could be sold and the proceeds used to buy something the school needs or perhaps be donated to an orphanage.

More, too, should be done to ensure that used books and magazines are sent where they are needed and not thrown into the dustbin. More city schools should adopt "sister" schools in rural areas and send used books to them. A group of mothers could so easily organize such activities, with a regular exchange of letters, pictures and news. The children on both sides would benefit—if only from a sense of widening horizons, a consciousness of a larger environment.

It is comforting to know that there are practical things we can easily do to help the environment, but we must also try to gain a broad understanding of the problem of pollution and its causes. For example, I only recently learned that part of the price we pay for white paper is the release of dioxins (including tetrachlorodiobenzodioxine, referred to as TCDD, one of the most dangerous chemicals ever produced) into rivers and seas, following a bleaching process using chlorine gas. The same process is used for white sanitary towels and white disposable nappies for babies. Pressure must be brought to bear on the mass media, to publish this sort of fact in as accessible a manner as possible. The lie that "white is clean" must be exposed. And, of course, alternative products must be made available. As women do most of the shopping for a household, they can help by boycotting items that they have learned are harmful to the environment.

From all over the world one can find examples of the good work being done to encourage and assist the preservation of the environment and uphold the balance of nature. Women in both the developed and developing countries are making their contribution, each according to her own individual talents, inclinations and opportunities. This is indeed heartwarming. One notable instance worth citing is the Green Belt Movement of Kenya, which promotes tree planting and agro-forestry. This not only helps sustain Kenya's eco-balance but also has the valuable side benefit of providing employment for women, for school-leavers and for the handicapped, in various fields, including the preparation and care of the seedling trees. The brain behind this Green Belt Movement is Professor Wangari, who has deservedly been described as one of the most dynamic women of Kenya's development scene.

In Turkey too, I am pleased to say, great efforts are being made to make people more environment-conscious. At Hacettepe University, a research centre is being set up within the Department of Geology to investigate and research environmental problems. There is also a Council for the Protection of the Environment within the Government, which attaches great importance to making the general public environment-conscious and aims to encourage people to play an active role in overcoming immediate environmental pollution and in preserving the balance of nature. Efforts are at present being concentrated on two pilot areas in Istanbul, and women in particular are being called upon to offer their services in this scheme.

Until recently it was economic and political issues that dominated international debate. Now it is the balance of nature that should be the prime concern. Here we all are, on this one planet Earth, sharing the same environment, and sharing the responsibility of making it better, not worse. The problems are daunting, but with knowledge, mutual encouragement and effort, I do believe that humankind collectively can do something towards solving them.

Chapter 16

DEVELOPMENT, POVERTY, ENVIRONMENT AND AID

John Vidal*

In the 1950s and 1960s there was the confident assumption that if you had enough aid money you could save the developing world. Today no aid can solve poverty. Aid does not help human development or the environment. Other mechanisms must be found to solve these problems. The 1990s are already the age of cruelty and oppression. Aid fatigue has set in. Every congressman in America agrees that it's pouring money down a black hole. It's a given that some aid is siphoned off, now watch it dry up ... Watch the march of the market economy. Look at the figures.

Only one point of view among many, perhaps, but no-one can doubt the figures any more. They are appalling, even compared with 10 years ago. At the second United Nations Conference on the Least Developed Countries, held in Paris in September 1990, the 41 least developed countries (LDCs) heard United Nations Secretary-General Javier Pérez de Cuéllar say that higher oil prices could wreck attempts to defeat famine which was threatening millions in Africa; that 30 per cent of all official development assistance (ODA) to their countries went on servicing debt; that it would need a trebling of the world's annual $12 billion ODA a year to achieve a 5 per cent growth rate by

*Environmental Editor, *The Guardian.*

the end of the decade; that food production for more than 400 million people has failed to match population growth; that per capita production has declined over the decade; that their share of world exports is now just 0.3 per cent compared with 1.4 per cent in 1980; that the transfer of resources to the developing countries has been reversed from a positive flow of $42.6 billion in 1981 to a negative flow of $32.5 billion in 1988; that the South was spending more and more of its income on armaments; that it's getting worse rather than better.

New modes for development

In public, politicians and economists agree that there have been blunders but argue that their first promise, though it sounds increasingly lame, still stands: that the traditional development models employed throughout the last 40 years are basically sound. The problem is still perceived by decision-makers to be one of cash, accountancy and economics. The world bodies argue courageously that if the world community gives more there will be less hardship. If the South industrializes, there will be wealth. Ergo, less poverty, less destruction of the environment, fewer empty bellies to feed and so on.

At the Antalya Round Table, many theories were expounded, solutions proposed, issues raised, and statements made, all sound more or less laudable, sensible and feasible in isolation. The world, it is said over and again, is in transition with new political and economic alignments, the technological revolution is in full flood and a surplus of wealth is, in theory, just waiting to be tapped, supposedly presenting limitless opportunities for the poor. In the words of Secretary-General Pérez de Cuéllar, "The international community will now turn in earnest to the betterment of the human condition. We are moving into a new era, a new society, more just and equitable."

The message then, as now, is that the end of the cold war and the spread of the market economy and democracy is the best thing for development since the Marshall Plan, a "Good Thing" for poverty and the environment, heralding "peace dividends" that will be used to increase the West's miserable contribution of 0.09 per cent of its gross domestic product (GDP) to world aid.

The theory still sounds fine but the peace dividend looks more than ever a fable. If Pérez de Cuéllar's words even then sounded wildly optimistic, today they would seem to be the stuff of dreams. One year on and the dividend has been all but exposed as a chimera, a marvellous opportunity high-jacked by politicians to invest in ever-more sophisticated weaponry. One year on and the Gulf war is forgotten but capital is still made from it by governments to justify anything they want except turn money spent on arms to the poor.

Poverty

As the walls of communism have tumbled, so the devastation wreaked for decades has been revealed and, rightly, the European Community and world bodies have turned to the environmental and infrastructural problems. Meanwhile, the poorest countries are further than ever from finding the means to solve their equally urgent problems. What is to become of Africa, ask people concerned for the continent, looking just a few years ahead at the inevitably enormous population explosion, the state of the cities, the decline in productive land, the internal wars and the increasing unpredictability of the rains. Where is the money to help them?

To one African in Antalya, the meeting is not quite real: "I have spent the morning," he said "listening to international bankers saying that if I had invested at the start of the 1980s my country would have been like Taiwan. Look, I just want money to rebuild the shelled-out schools, to provide primary health care." Even to eminent economists in Antalya there is a problem: it is always a bit embarrassing when the developed world excludes the Third World from discussions.

The flip side of the rhetoric is brutal, and few people even in the most educated, sophisticated circles, are yet prepared to consider it. It is that the very poor, two thirds of the world now and up to four fifths by the end of the decade if the poverty spiral isn't arrested, will increasingly play no part in the economy of the developed North. In economic jargon there will be "delinkage" with no spillover of international "wealth". The abysmally poor will get abysmally poorer and be left to fend for themselves. Instead of the 1990s being the decade of democracy and development, it becomes the one in which the North waves a bitter goodbye to the South.

In economic terms, the spectre is real. Here, talking in private, is an international financier at the same UNDP birthday party, trying to attract money to Poland—by no means the worst off of countries: "The market economy, with its vast amounts of capital swirling around for those with credible business plans in favoured strategic countries, is not the slightest bit interested in investing in hopeless cases when it knows it can earn huge returns in the North. That said there's an unreality and arrogance in some former communist countries. They believe the whole world is focused on their little countries. They are going to be very disappointed." And here's a Saudi replying tersely to the question of why more petrodollars were not invested in the South: "Simply, because it is safer in the North." And with that logic the war, a few months later was fought.

Few reminders are needed of the damage done—still being done—in the Gulf. In the fight for the security of one resource, every other resource known to man was employed to wreak massive destruction. Yet for all the political justification given for combat, the possible environmental consequences were all but ignored before the outbreak of hostilities. Never mind the rights and wrongs of the war, or the terrible costs involved, which, if used wisely, would have gone so far to alleviating the suffering elsewhere, just as a symbol of humanity laying waste to nature, or as a metaphor for the rich destroying the poor, it was perfect.

Meanwhile, the logging and the mining and the transfer of resources from poor to rich continues, buoyed by a world economy which stacks the cards against the developing nations. Industry, culprit or saviour, certainly has a huge potential for technological innovations to improve their environmental performance and factors of three and four over the next 50 years a reduction of overall environmental impact per unit of GDP by 65–75 per cent are commonly quoted. But a global economy growing at a modest 2–3 per cent a year implies a quadrupling of industrial output in the same period so that a fourfold increase in environmental performance is necessary just to keep today's environmental impacts constant. And the scientific evidence increasingly suggests that these impacts portend future disasters. The bankers and the financiers in Antalya are largely worldly, if not wise. "Two hundred years ago Britain had a population of what, 10 million? Now it's 60 million. Whoever then thought your country could sustain that many people?", one of them asks. He is not at all impressed with arguments that Britain can cope only at the expense of poorer countries.

Environment linkages

Ever so slowly, though, through the offices of the UNDP and others, the message gets through and public concern in the North is starting to spill over to the South as the links between environment and development, environment and poverty, environment and war, environment and health are made. But the environment is still not yet perceived in political circles as the central issue it should be. How can it be, when politicians think in terms of a few years and environmentalists in decades or more? Bizarrely, many of the answers may have to come from global industry which, at its best, has to think far ahead to maintain its profits.

"There is simply no future for the planet without a global war on poverty," says Maurice Strong, Secretary General of the United Nations Conference on Environment and Development on his last day in Antalya. "It's just not feasible for the resource base and the environment to be maintained when people are being forced, through poverty, to destroy the base on which they depend. The poor know what they are doing. People in the First World think of population in the South as the problem, but they are reluctant to realize that it's their wasteful industrial civilization that's forcing the South into this situation." Unfortunately, he is talking to others who well understand the issues.

The eminent economists are meeting on their own in Antalya. They miss some fundamental global points, as no doubt do the environmentalists, but just for the record, they might have appreciated Carl Tham of the Swedish International Development Authority: "Poverty is often a result of environmental degradation," he says. Soil erosion, deforestation, water pollution, desertification and the salinization of irrigated land all work against people's potential as producers. Environmental degradation exposes the poorest to greatest risks. The famines in Ethiopia and the floods in Bangladesh have their roots in extensive environmental degradation. There are millions of environmental refugees who have fled from their homes often putting greater stress on cities because nature can no longer feed them. At the same time, poverty is the cause of environmental degradation. The shortage of land, caused by population growth often itself a consequence of poverty leads to an expansion of cultivation in ecologically sensitive areas. Poverty means limited knowledge about alternative methods, it means limited political influence to halt unacceptable development.

Development, poverty, environment. Where, then, aid in the new world? For a bleak view, here's an English professor, talking in private. "There is still a role for foreign assistance, plenty of scope for generosity. The corruption of aid is not corruption in the legal sense but in its insidious ways of making countries dependent. When donors claim generosity, it is really self-interest."

Conclusion

Self-interest, finally, has to be the bottom line. For the rich it's defending insanely low energy standards, trade agreements, industrial, banking and accountancy practices. It's defending the colonial activities of its industries abroad, accepting the status quo over pollution, timber imports, water quality, trade, debt agreements or whatever. If there is to be change, and surely there has to be a radical rethink before change is forced on great areas of the world, it has to start with the privileged for accepting their global responsibilities. That requires not so much money but a new awareness, serious dialogue and, above all commitment. A decade of that and global poverty might look very different.

Chapter 17

A NEW
EARTH ORDER

Claes Nobel*

I have a vision. I have a vision of a new kind of world. A world that is better, safer and saner than the one we presently know. It is a vision of a rebirth for the Earth. A rebirth into a new and sustainable future, in which people will live in harmony with each other and in harmony with the Earth. It is a vision solidly founded upon common sense and common action for our common future.

For the sake of global survival it is my most sincere hope that people around the world will soon recognize the need to embrace and to share with others an environmentally positive vision of a new earth order. A vision of a new future, built upon the bedrock qualities of reverence for life and service to the earth.

Need for action

As the twentieth century draws to a close, our world is beset with great difficulties and much human suffering. The complexity and severity of the present crisis is widespread and deep-rooted. The compounded impact of discord and pain is of an unparalleled magnitude and never, in recorded history, has such wholesale destruction of our environment taken place.

*Chairman of United Earth and founder of the Earth Prize. This paper is based on speeches delivered by Mr. Nobel and edited by Üner Kirdar for this book.

This is tragic. Tragic because, with resolve based upon ethics, many of the problems we are burdened with and most of the issues we so desperately are trying to come to grips with could have been avoided. To its great perplexity, the world is realizing that a severe deterioration is taking place in the quality of life, for both nature and humanity.

I am neither a pessimist nor an optimist, I consider myself to be a realist. In that capacity, I state most emphatically that we humans must drastically change the way we treat our environment and the way we interrelate with it.

A great global transformation is called for. Without further procrastination, immediate and fundamental changes must take place in human values, priorities, behaviour and lifestyles. We have to undertake such measures of change and self-discipline to avoid a total collapse of our cultures, civilizations and environment. Indeed, upon such a change depends our very future. Otherwise, we cannot expect to survive.

The severity and the urgency of the present crises are so critical and so profound that every human being, regardless of race, creed, nationality or occupation, must fully accept, that the future of the planet is in our hands, in the hands of each and every capable individual on earth. The survival of the planet depends on the effort of the individual. Therefore, I state: think globally, act locally and commit individually. Individually we can each make a small difference, but together we can all make an enormous difference. Therefore, I state: now is the time for people to act as Earth Trustees.

Earth is a planet of oneness, a planet of wholeness, and a planet of balance. Earth is a living fragile planet and life is the common thread that links together all creation on Earth. On Earth, everything is interconnected, interrelated and interdependent. Now, there is a dawning of consciousness that we are all indeed a united Earth.

The world needs a new guiding vision, a new idea, one that will catch on like a brush fire, one that will bring true inspiration to all the people in all the corners of the world, by giving them new, realistic hope—a vision that can be embraced and transformed into worldwide action by youth and adults alike, a vision that will attract new and vigorous leadership, a vision that will materialize into the "New Earth Order".

This transformation must take place. The catalysts for change will be many. I believe that in establishing the new earth order for the third millennium, the following five catalysts will be among the most powerful and instrumental: the power of business; the power of the media; the power of women; the power of youth; and the power of earth ethics.

The five catalysts

The first area, the power of business, involves the leaders of business, industry and commerce. The leaders of marketing, of advertising, of public relations and so on. The individuals and the corporations who recognize the environmental challenge and who grasp the many new opportunities that are associated therewith will do well. The general public, their customers, are now reacting—they are becoming increasingly environmentally concerned and environmentally active.

The general public will increasingly demand environmental responsibility, environmental accountability and a change to a new world order, one that is based upon common sense and common action for our common future.

To that extent, organic and natural food from sustainable agriculture will flourish, as will products that meet environmental standards both in manufacturing—and in recycling. Waste will be turned into useful products: on an industrial basis, for example, garbage and sewage will be recycled into compost. There will be seals of environmental approval like Germany's "Blue Angel", which has already been in effect for twelve years. These seals will evaluate services and products through criteria such as the use of energy and of natural resource, and the pollution involved in the manufacture, use and disposal of the product.

The second area of great hope is the media. The media will play a very great role in shaping our future by informing, educating and building opinions. And, most important of all, this modern electronic miracle, which instantly reaches all the corners of the world, will increasingly continue to expose products, services and actions that will either improve or degrade the environment. In the spotlight of public media exposure, or with the possibility of media exposure, many actions of environmental irresponsibility will be contained and corrected. The media can thus dispel environmental atrocities, just like sunlight dispels darkness. Also, the media will stimulate and bring about environmental responsibility and environmental action.

The third area of hope is the power of women. Women will have a very significant role in building a new world, characterized by new values, new priorities and new and greater amounts of common sense. Unquestionably and unfortunately, we still live in a world that is basically governed by men. Men are the ones who make most of the decisions in politics, religion, business, health and education. Is it possible to create a viable planet and to have a sound future if we do not have mutual and equal representation and input from both sexes? The world particularly needs the input of women, for they represent the very gender that gives birth to new life. Therefore, for the sake of global survival men and women must, in this decade, become equal and cooperative partners in creating the common good for our common future.

The fourth area of great hope is the power of youth. Today, youth represents 50 per cent of the world population, and 100 per cent of our future. Until now, youth has seldom made its voice heard in the affairs of the world. However, through the media young people are becoming increasingly informed about the state of the world. Youth has no preconceived ideas. Young minds are not cast in concrete and will not accept matters as they presently are. They will demand a change. They will undertake the change—they are the change.

The fifth area of hope is the power of earth-ethics. Earth-ethics constitutes the totality of an individual's right relationship and ethical behaviour: towards himself or herself; towards family, friends and neighbours; towards the environment; towards plants, animals and Nature. Earth-ethics is the moral way to a better, safer and saner world. To practice earth ethics is to express truth in thought, word and deed.

Conclusion

These five areas hold a realistic and true hope for turning the many different areas of crisis into lasting harmony. They hold the hope for creating for us all a better, safer and saner world.

Despite the many exceedingly serious threats presently jeopardizing the well-being of our environment, it is through these five forces that we can mobilize both the resource and the massive amounts of "Right Action", to avoid a total collapse of our life-support systems.

These five specific catalysts are the sources of great hope and great power, through which each and every one of us will fill a major role in the world's forthcoming efforts to establishing a sustainable environment.

Chapter 18

A NEW
WORLD STRATEGY
FOR ECOLOGICAL
BALANCE

Sasha White*

We stand at a point in the history of humanity and our Earth when we have no viable choice but to join together in global cooperation and teamwork. We have made progress in many areas, but we are falling behind. The problems the world faces today—global warming, overpopulation, desertification and the rest—seem to be outstripping civilization's capacity to deal with them.

Governments have long struggled with these challenges. Now, the time has come for all citizens to take a more active role. Individuals must contribute and take responsibility for helping to develop viable solutions. Global team work must be initiated to implement these solutions.

Technical "fixes" and business as usual have long since ceased to be enough. Man must now learn to live in harmony with nature in order to create a sustainable society. A sustainable society is one whose demands upon the Earth do not diminish the lives of future generations. Can we do what has to be done to create one?

Many people, especially environmentalists, believe it is too late. "If everyone stopped driving their cars this very moment and did every-

---

*Founder, Campaign for the Earth, San Francisco, whose original strategy paper has been edited by Üner Kirdar for this book.

thing we know we should, we are 10–15 years behind in reversing the situation", says one environmentalist. My philosophy, however, is that the environmental crisis is a blessing in disguise. It takes what it takes to get our attention! And, if this is what has to happen to bring us together, then I believe the unifying crisis of the environment is part of the plan for humanity on Earth. There is something within me that knows we were not put on this planet for doom and gloom. Even from a common sense standpoint, if we are able to achieve as much in the environmental arena in the next 20 years as has been achieved with technology and communications during the past 20 years, there is a good chance that we can create a sustainable world.

Humanity now is faced with the supreme challenge: do we continue with our old ways or do we create a new world strategy? While tremendous efforts and strategies are being implemented throughout the globe, there has never been one unifying movement to join all forces into one massive worldwide team.

Need for a new strategy

Global warming is the greatest social, political, economic and environmental challenge we face for the 1990s and beyond. This issue will be, indeed must be, a strong inducer of interdependence among peoples and nations. Even a precursory glance at some of the other statistics is frightening: every minute of each day, 18 children under the age of five die of starvation; 150 million more people will get skin cancer in the United States alone over the next 80 years if nothing is done to save the ozone layer; we are losing rain forests at the rate of one football field a second; nearly 20 billion people have inadequate drinking water, and 3 billion lack proper sanitation; about 2 billion tons of waste a year from factories, homes and farms end up in the sea; as many as a million species may vanish by the year 2000; the world's population is exploding and depleting non-renewable resources; $2.5 billion dollars a day of our world's resources are spent on the military.

We have enough technology to solve every problem we are facing on our planet. There is enough food to feed every mouth. What we must do is accept personal responsibility and come together. At this moment in time, we have the wisdom and the knowledge to solve, through real methods, every challenge facing humanity, and the planet Earth. What we need is a new strategy for the environment.

If we do not implement a new world strategy for the environment, we will be reduced to using previous reactive strategies and the health of the planet will continue to deteriorate.

A new business strategy

The world needs to conduct its business in a new way. The present dominant economic system teaches people to perceive the richness of their lives in terms of how many material goods they consume. This is contrary to what the teachers of the world's religious traditions have told us. Our system of trade in the market place factors in the costs and benefits to the parties of the transaction but disregards the interests of bystanders. The way we calculate the economic growth with which the world is obsessed fails to count as costs the degradation of our living planet and the exhaustion of its resources. We became like heirs squandering a legacy it took aeons to a cumulate. As only money talks in the market-place, the whims of the rich are carefully tended while the necessities of the poor are neglected. Thus, while dozens of tranquillizers are available to the wealthy, pharmaceutical companies have no interest in developing medicines to treat the tropical maladies that disfigure the lives of millions of impoverished people. Giant corporations some of the most powerful actors in our world are effectively on automatic pilot in the blind pursuit of profit, beyond genuine human control. The owners, i.e., the stockholders, lack real power while the managers are a self-perpetuating group selected according to the corporate system's own criteria. In more and more people's lives, the most influential teacher is a system of advertising—a teacher whose most distinguishing characteristic is that it treats its students wholly as a means to its own ends, seeking not to enrich their lives but to persuade them to part with their money, for whatever reason. Nations strive against each other for advantage in the market-place with the same fervour, with much the same anxiety for security, and with rather similar skewing effects on social choices, as they strive in the arms race.

If we continue on our present course, our lives will be even fuller of material things but emptier of those human bonds of friendship and community and cultural meanings that make our lives truly rich; we will bequeath unto our children, and their children, a poisoned and denuded Earth. As our grasp of what is really of value in human life weakens, we will become more willing to let the market with its skewed vision mould our world view and govern our destiny.

With a more balanced approach to our economic life, our islands of private wealth could be better integrated into a coherent, wider human community. Our measures of economic progress would take into account the condition in which we are passing down to our descendants the heritage of our natural environment. Resources would go to meet the most pressing human needs, including those of the poor, who are mute in the market place. We would be more able, both as individuals and as nations, to choose how we want to live our lives, not from a sense of compulsion, but freely, out of our own vision.

A transformation of business as part of this new world strategy would find the priorities of business dramatically shifted. Rather than linking actions primarily to short-term sales and profits, companies would set goals from broader, long-range perspectives, including their contribution to the global ecology and with concern for the general and spiritual well-being of their owner/operators since the employee-owned corporation is the business form of the future. Employee-owned corporations naturally make kinder and gentler decisions. As they proliferate, there will be less and less unemployment since their highest goals will become the enhancement of human satisfaction rather than mere monetary profit.

If we are to save our environment, some sort of ecological impact taxation on business appears necessary. To be effective, such taxes and other government interventions will have to be global in scope. These transnational taxes and regulations will be popularly supported as common sense solutions only as people begin to think for themselves rather than surrendering to the fear-based chantings of extreme liberals or backward-looking conservative politicians. A basic foundation for such common-sense thinking will be much more open access to unbiased statistics and information. Providing this information in lively ways will be the largest growth industry of the 1990s.

With the untruth that we live in a world where there is not enough for all being replaced by acceptance that there are plenty of resources for everyone, combined with transformed enterprises exercising their enlightened, caring ways of doing business, economic conditions of abundant prosperity will emerge. The strategy currently underlying the governance of peoples and their political processes is based upon an outdated understanding of power. It reflects the limits of a species that has been preoccupied with physical survival throughout its evolution. Our species has now entered a new phase in its evolution.

Although physical survival remains the primary focus of millions of humans, our species, as a whole, has learned how to feed and clothe itself. Physical survival alone is no longer sufficient. It is now necessary to address the deeper and more meaningful issues of the human spirit.

The key to our physical survival, as well as our continued evolution, rests with our ability to recognize that a threshold without precedent has been crossed and that we must accommodate the new circumstances that confront us. Until now, power has been understood as the ability to manipulate and control the environment and others. This is power over the external world. Individuals and nations most able to dominate others were perceived as the most powerful, and the most important in their hierarchies. Within political hierarchies and food chains, the power and importance attributed to higher positions in relation to lower positions reflect the perception of power as external.

A new type of power is emerging in the political arena. It comes from the alignment of decisions and actions with the highest aspects of the human psyche—those that reach toward harmony, cooperation, sharing and reverence for life. We are making the transition from a species that pursues external power—the power to manipulate and

control—to a species that pursues authentic power, i.e., conscious alignment with the most noble characteristics of the human spirit. We have
no choice. The pursuit of external power, which served our evolution
through hundreds of millennia, now produces only violence and destruction. Violence between nuclear adversaries is no longer an acceptable
option. Violence to the environment is no longer an acceptable option.

If a New World Strategy based upon harmony, cooperation, sharing, and reverence for life is not created and implemented quickly, the
physical survival of our species, and the ecological system of life of
which our species is a part, will face certain disaster. At least some of the
fifty thousand nuclear warheads that our species possesses will be used,
despite the collapse of the cold war. Global deterioration of the environment will result in species-wide catastrophe for humanity, and hundreds of thousands of other species.

The earth and personal growth

The essential strategy underlying all strategies is that one person can
make a difference. If we join together in action, we will increase the
potential of beneficial, meaningful change. Strategy needs to be aimed
at evoking concern and commitment. We must believe in our potential
for change. Role models can provide a glimpse of one's own potential.
A role model who acts with initiative and compassion empowers the
individual to the highest potential. What can be achieved begins in the
imagination and is activated by inspiration. Personal growth is inevitable when there is growth in consciousness and empowerment. We live
in a dysfunctional world. Civil unrest, poverty, malnutrition, crime,
violence, drug use, starvation and war are part of everyday life in all
parts of the world. Clearly, human rights issues underlie these social
problems. Political oppression, the lack of adequate food, housing and
medical resources and unequal opportunities for employment and education sow the seeds of discontent. At the root of these issues, we find
racism, unresolved ethnic conflict and worldwide imbalance in wealth
and resources.

A world that permits these problems faces continued civil unrest and war as people fight for their rights. It faces continued demoralization of large numbers of people as they lose hope and turn to crime, violence and the use of drugs. The cost in personal suffering is immeasurable. The cost to individual nations and to the world is incalculable, as resources are drained by strife and war and huge sums must be spent on social and remedial programmes. In the new, interdependent world that is emerging, these issues become even more crucial, because dysfunction in any part, within a nation or within a particular world region, will impede prosperity and progress for everyone.

Conclusion

A world that works together to share resources and ensure everyone's civil, political, economic and social rights eliminates many of the causes of social unrest, poverty, starvation and war. The achievement of human rights leads to peace and prosperity. Significant numbers of people become contributing members of society, so that economies grow and standards of living rise. More resources then become available for public services, public works, health care, environmental protection and basic research. Cultural and educational standards rise. As suffering is lessened, individual physical and psychological well being is enhanced and the overall quality of life improves. A positive cycle is created that benefits everyone.

Let us create a new world strategy for a balanced ecology so that we can make our vision a reality.

VOLUME II
ECONOMIC CHANGE

VOLUME III
GLOBALIZATION OF MARKETS

UNDP DEVELOPMENT STUDY PROGRAMME

The Development Study Programme of the United Nations Development Programme (UNDP) was established by the Governing Council of UNDP in 1981, in order to:

- Promote a greater understanding of the issues concerning development and technical cooperation;
- Strengthen public and governmental support for development and technical cooperation;
- Generate new ideas and innovative solutions to the problems of development and technical cooperation;
- Mobilize additional resources for development and technical cooperation.

The activities of the UNDP Development Study Programme take different forms such as seminars, lectures and informal discussion groups. Participants at the various events held under the auspices of the Programme are drawn from among high-level national policy makers, government representatives, senior officials of the United Nations system, leaders of public and private enterprises and representatives of the media and academics.

The UNDP Development Study Programme is financed from voluntary contributions of Governments, as well as international public and private institutions and foundations. Contributions may include the provision of hosting facilities and collaboration in organizing joint seminars and meetings.

William H. Draper III is the Administrator of UNDP and Üner Kirdar is the Director of UNDP Development Study Programme.

UNDP Headquarters is at One UN Plaza, New York, New York, 10017

ABOUT THE EDITOR

Üner **Kirdar** is currently the Director of the UNDP Development Study Programme; he has been the Director of the Division of External Relations and Secretary to the Governing Council Secretariat of UNDP since 1980.

Born in Turkey on 1 January 1933, he graduated from the Faculty of Law, Istanbul, undertook post-graduate studies at the London School of Economics, and received his Ph.D. from Jesus College, University of Cambridge, England.

Dr. Kirdar has served the United Nations system in various capacities, such as Secretary of the Preparatory Committee and United Nations Conference on Human Settlements (1974–1976), Secretary of the Group of Experts on the Structure of the United Nations System (1975), and a Senior Officer for Inter-Agency Affairs in the Office of the United Nations Secretary-General (1972–1977).

He has been the main architect of the UNDP Development Study Programme and has organized several seminars, round-table meetings, lectures and discussion groups attended by high-level national and international policy makers.

He has also held senior positions in the Ministry of Foreign Affairs of Turkey, including Director for International Economic Organizations and Deputy Permanent Representative of Turkey to the United Nations Office at Geneva.

Dr. Kirdar is the author of the book *Structure of UN Economic Aid to Underdeveloped Countries*, Martinus Nijhoff, (1966; 1968). He is the co-editor and contributor to other books: *Human Development: The Neglected Dimension* (1986); *Human Development, Adjustment and Growth* (1987); *Managing Human Development* (1988); *Development for People* (1989); *Equality of Opportunity Within and Among Nations*, Praeger Publishers, (1977); "Human Resources Development: Challenge for the '80s", *Crisis of The '80s*, (1983); "Impact of IMF Conditionality on Human Conditions", *Adjustment with Growth* (1984); *The Lingering Debt Crisis* (1985). He has also contributed numerous articles to professional books and journals.